Amazon S3 Cookbook

Over 30 hands-on recipes that will get you up and running
with Amazon Simple Storage Service (S3) efficiently

Naoya Hashimoto

professional expertise distilled

BIRMINGHAM - MUMBAI

Amazon S3 Cookbook

First published: August 2015

Production reference: 1240815

Published by Packt Publishing Ltd.
Livery Place
35 Livery Street
Birmingham B3 2PB, UK.

ISBN 978-1-78528-070-2

www.packtpub.com

Credits

Author

Naoya Hashimoto

Reviewers

Venugopal Jidigam

Hitesh Kumar

Robert Mitwicki

Commissioning Editor

Amarabha Banerjee

Acquisition Editor

Reshma Raman

Content Development Editor

Mamta Walkar

Technical Editor

Vivek Arora

Copy Editors

Merilyn Pereira

Laxmi Subramanian

Project Coordinator

Shipra Chawhan

Proofreader

Safis Editing

Indexer

Rekha Nair

Production Coordinator

Melwyn Dsa

Cover Work

Melwyn Dsa

About the Author

Naoya Hashimoto has worked on system designing, implementing, and system maintenance as an infrastructure engineer in a data center, a management service provider, and housing/hosting service provider for years. After he was introduced to public cloud services a few years ago, his career, interest, and motive shifted to the public cloud, including private- and hybrid-cloud-computing-related services (such as network, storage, orchestration, job automation, and monitoring), as well as to open source software.

He has been a technical reviewer of many books, such as *Mastering AWS Development*, *Icinga Network Monitoring*, *PostgreSQL Cookbook*, and *Building Networks and Servers Using Beaglebone*, all by Packt Publishing.

I would like to thank Toshi Asaba, the general manager at GDI Communications (where I work), for being understanding and for his generous support in the publishing of this book.

About the Reviewers

Venugopal Jidigam is the director of engineering at WaveMaker (a Pramati venture) and has built a cloud platform based on AWS and Docker that hosts the online RAD Studio. Prior to WaveMaker, he served in several roles as a product consultant, working with Tibco on ActiveMatrix and Progress Software to build their Savvion BPM suite. Venugopal started his career by working on the Pramati app server and gained expertise in building enterprise software and highly scalable systems.

Hitesh Kumar has 3 years of software development experience and has worked on problems related to machine learning and big data. Prior to this, he completed his undergraduate degree in computer science. His interest lies in solving the fundamental problems that plague our society.

Robert Mitwicki has been a software architect and developer since 2006, when he started his first company. He is a big fan of the open source community and contributes to it. He has experience in software design, quality assurance, software engineering, and DevOps practices, which he gathered by working with companies, such as Logica Poland, Popla, FXI Technolgies, Monterail, and Salomon Automation. Robert is also a cofounder of Patterm and Opensoftware.pl (http://opensoftware.pl/).

www.PacktPub.com

Support files, eBooks, discount offers, and more

For support files and downloads related to your book, please visit www.PacktPub.com.

Did you know that Packt offers eBook versions of every book published, with PDF and ePub files available? You can upgrade to the eBook version at www.PacktPub.com and as a print book customer, you are entitled to a discount on the eBook copy. Get in touch with us at service@packtpub.com for more details.

At www.PacktPub.com, you can also read a collection of free technical articles, sign up for a range of free newsletters and receive exclusive discounts and offers on Packt books and eBooks.

https://www2.packtpub.com/books/subscription/packtlib

Do you need instant solutions to your IT questions? PacktLib is Packt's online digital book library. Here, you can search, access, and read Packt's entire library of books.

Why subscribe?

- ▶ Fully searchable across every book published by Packt
- ▶ Copy and paste, print, and bookmark content
- ▶ On demand and accessible via a web browser

Free access for Packt account holders

If you have an account with Packt at www.PacktPub.com, you can use this to access PacktLib today and view 9 entirely free books. Simply use your login credentials for immediate access.

Instant updates on new Packt books

Get notified! Find out when new books are published by following @PacktEnterprise on Twitter or the *Packt Enterprise* Facebook page.

Table of Contents

Preface

Amazon Simple Storage Service (Amazon S3) is one of the most popular online object storage services with high scalability, durability, and automatic self-healing. It also enables programmatic access with AWS SDKs that simplify your programming tasks.

Amazon S3 Cookbook is a recipe-based practical guide that will get you up and running with using Amazon S3 efficiently. This book will not only tell you how to use several functions of Amazon S3, but it will also give you valuable information and a deeper understanding of, for example, managing buckets and objects with AWS SDKs, cost calculation, how to secure your contents, lifecycle management, and performance optimization to leverage Amazon S3 to build amazing cloud-based apps.

What this book covers

Chapter 1, Managing Common Operations with AWS SDKs, introduces what AWS SDKs can do with Amazon S3 by using the official AWS SDK sample application code to create S3 buckets and upload, list, get, and download objects into and from a bucket.

Chapter 2, Hosting a Static Website on Amazon S3 Bucket, covers hosting a static website's contents by using a custom domain on Amazon S3 instead of using web servers such as Apache or Nginx on EC2 through a management console (GUI) and AWS CLI (command line). You will also learn the merits of using Amazon S3 as a website.

Chapter 3, Calculating Cost with the AWS Simple Monthly Calculator, talks about calculating the total cost of storing data and delivering objects through S3 with the Amazon Web Services Simple Monthly Calculator (the AWS calculator), based on a couple of scenarios.

Chapter 4, Deploying a Static Website with CloudFormation, covers deploying a template of a static website with CloudFormation via the S3 console and using AWS CLI.

Chapter 5, Distributing Your Contents via CloudFront, talks about delivering a static website on S3 buckets through the CloudFront edge location (CDN), configuring S3 buckets as an origin store to minimize network latency.

Chapter 6, Securing Resources with Bucket Policies and IAM, covers managing access to resources such as buckets and objects, configuring bucket policies, and IAM users, groups, and policies.

Chapter 7, Sending Authenticated Requests with AWS SDKs, talks about making requests using IAM and federated users' temporary credentials with AWS SDKs to grant permissions to temporarily access Amazon S3 resources.

Chapter 8, Protecting Data Using Server-side and Client-side Encryption, deals with encrypting and decrypting your data using server-side and client-side encryption to securely upload and download your contents.

Chapter 9, Enabling Cross-origin Resource Sharing, shows you how to enable cross-origin resource sharing (CORS) and allow cross-origin access to S3 resources to interact with resources in a different domain for client web applications.

Chapter 10, Managing Object Lifecycle to Lower the Cost, talks about configuring lifetime cycle policies on S3 buckets to automatically delete after a certain time, using Reduced Redundancy Storage (RRS) or by archiving objects into Amazon Glacier.

Chapter 11, S3 Performance Optimization, deals with improving the performance of uploading, downloading, and getting and listing objects.

Chapter 12, Creating Triggers and Notifying S3 Events to Lambda, covers sending notifications to let AWS Lambda execute Lambda functions that enable S3 event notifications.

What you need for this book

The following packages are required to install and use AWS CLI:

- ▸ Python 2.7 or later
- ▸ pip

For *Chapter 1, Managing Common Operations with AWS SDKs*, the following packages are required to install several AWS SDKs. The details are introduced in each section:

- ▸ J2SE Development Kit 6.0 or later for AWS SDK for Java
- ▸ Node.js for AWS SDK for Node.js
- ▸ Python 2.6 or 2.7 for AWS SDK for Python (Boto)
- ▸ Ruby for AWS SDK for Ruby V2
- ▸ PHP for AWS SDK for PHP

Who this book is for

This book is for cloud developers who have experience of using Amazon S3 and are also familiar with Amazon S3.

Sections

In this book, you will find several headings that appear frequently (Getting ready, How to do it, How it works, There's more, and See also).

To give clear instructions on how to complete a recipe, we use these sections as follows:

Getting ready

This section tells you what to expect in the recipe, and describes how to set up any software or any preliminary settings required for the recipe.

How to do it...

This section contains the steps required to follow the recipe.

How it works...

This section usually consists of a detailed explanation of what happened in the previous section.

There's more...

This section consists of additional information about the recipe in order to make the reader more knowledgeable about the recipe.

See also

This section provides helpful links to other useful information for the recipe.

Conventions

In this book, you will find a number of text styles that distinguish between different kinds of information. Here are some examples of these styles and an explanation of their meaning.

Code words in text, database table names, folder names, filenames, file extensions, pathnames, dummy URLs, user input, and Twitter handles are shown as follows: "We can include other contexts through the use of the `include` directive."

A block of code is set as follows:

```
{
"Version":"2012-10-17",
"Statement":[{
"Sid":"PublicReadGetObjects",
"Effect":"Allow",
"Principal": "*",
"Action":["s3:GetObject"],
"Resource":["arn:aws:s3:::<your_bucket>/*"]
}]
}
```

When we wish to draw your attention to a particular part of a code block, the relevant lines or items are set in bold:

```
$ aws s3 sync <your_document_directory>/ s3://<your_bucket> --region
<region_name>
```

Example:

```
$ aws s3 syncmy_doc_dir/ s3://hashnao.info --region ap-northeast-1
```

Any command-line input or output is written as follows:

```
$ dig hashweb.s3-website-ap-northeast-1.amazonaws.com

; <<>>DiG 9.8.3-P1 <<>> hashweb.s3-website-ap-northeast-1.amazonaws.com
;; global options: +cmd
;; Got answer:
;; ->>HEADER<<- opcode: QUERY, status: NOERROR, id: 45068
;; flags: qrrdra; QUERY: 1, ANSWER: 2, AUTHORITY: 4,
```

New terms and **important words** are shown in bold. Words that you see on the screen, for example, in menus or dialog boxes, appear in the text like this: "Click on **Static Website Hosting** and then select **Enable website hosting**."

[Warnings or important notes appear in a box like this.]

[Tips and tricks appear like this.]

Reader feedback

Feedback from our readers is always welcome. Let us know what you think about this book—what you liked or disliked. Reader feedback is important for us as it helps us develop titles that you will really get the most out of.

To send us general feedback, simply e-mail `feedback@packtpub.com`, and mention the book's title in the subject of your message.

If there is a topic that you have expertise in and you are interested in either writing or contributing to a book, see our author guide at `www.packtpub.com/authors`.

Customer support

Now that you are the proud owner of a Packt book, we have a number of things to help you to get the most from your purchase.

Downloading the example code

You can download the example code files from your account at `http://www.packtpub.com` for all the Packt Publishing books you have purchased. If you purchased this book elsewhere, you can visit `http://www.packtpub.com/support` and register to have the files e-mailed directly to you.

Errata

Although we have taken every care to ensure the accuracy of our content, mistakes do happen. If you find a mistake in one of our books—maybe a mistake in the text or the code—we would be grateful if you could report this to us. By doing so, you can save other readers from frustration and help us improve subsequent versions of this book. If you find any errata, please report them by visiting `http://www.packtpub.com/submit-errata`, selecting your book, clicking on the **Errata Submission Form** link, and entering the details of your errata. Once your errata are verified, your submission will be accepted and the errata will be uploaded to our website or added to any list of existing errata under the Errata section of that title.

To view the previously submitted errata, go to `https://www.packtpub.com/books/content/support` and enter the name of the book in the search field. The required information will appear under the **Errata** section.

Piracy

Piracy of copyrighted material on the Internet is an ongoing problem across all media. At Packt, we take the protection of our copyright and licenses very seriously. If you come across any illegal copies of our works in any form on the Internet, please provide us with the location address or website name immediately so that we can pursue a remedy.

Please contact us at `copyright@packtpub.com` with a link to the suspected pirated material.

We appreciate your help in protecting our authors and our ability to bring you valuable content.

Questions

If you have a problem with any aspect of this book, you can contact us at `questions@packtpub.com`, and we will do our best to address the problem.

1
Managing Common Operations with AWS SDKs

We will cover the basic operations of AWS SDKs to understand what they can do with Amazon S3 with the official AWS SDK sample application code to create S3 buckets, and upload, list, get, and download objects into and from a bucket.

In this chapter, we will cover:

- ▶ Learning AWS SDK for Java and basic S3 operations with sample code
- ▶ Learning AWS SDK for Node.js and basic S3 operations with sample code
- ▶ Learning AWS SDK for Python and basic S3 operations with sample code
- ▶ Learning AWS SDK for Ruby and basic S3 operations with sample code
- ▶ Learning AWS SDK for PHP and basic S3 operations with sample code

Introduction

Amazon Simple Storage Service (Amazon S3) is a cloud object storage service provided by Amazon Web Services. As Amazon S3 does not have a minimum fee, we just pay for what we store. We can store and get any amount of data, known as objects, in S3 buckets in different geographical regions through API or several SDKs. AWS SDKs provide programmatic access, for example, multiply uploading objects, versioning objects, configuring object access lists, and so on.

Amazon Web Services provides the following SDKs at `http://aws.amazon.com/developers/getting-started/`:

▸ AWS SDK for Android

▸ AWS SDK for JavaScript (Browser)

▸ AWS SDK for iOS

▸ AWS SDK for Java

▸ AWS SDK for .NET

▸ AWS SDK for Node.js

▸ AWS SDK for PHP

▸ AWS SDK for Python

▸ AWS SDK for Ruby

Learning AWS SDK for Java and basic S3 operations with sample code

This section tells you about how to configure an IAM user to access S3 and install AWS SDK for Java. It also talks about how to create S3 buckets, put objects, and get objects using the sample code. It explains how the sample code runs as well.

Getting ready

AWS SDK for Java is a Java API for AWS and contains AWS the Java library, code samples, and Eclipse IDE support. You can easily build scalable applications by working with Amazon S3, Amazon Glacier, and more.

To get started with AWS SDK for Java, it is necessary to install the following on your development machine:

▸ J2SE Development Kit 6.0 or later

▸ Apache Maven

How to do it...

First, we set up an IAM user, create a user policy, and attach the policy to the IAM user in the IAM management console in order to securely allow the IAM user to access the S3 bucket. We can define the access control for the IAM user by configuring the IAM policy. Then, we install AWS SDK for Java by using Apache Maven and git.

For more information about AWS **Identity and Access Management** (**IAM**), refer to http://aws.amazon.com/iam/.

There are two ways to install AWS SDK for Java, one is to get the source code from GitHub, and the other is to use Apache Maven. We use the latter because the official site recommends this way and it is much easier.

1. Sign in to the AWS management console and move to the IAM console at https://console.aws.amazon.com/iam/home.

2. In the navigation panel, click on **Users** and then on **Create New Users**.

3. Enter the username and select **Generate an access key for each user**, then click on **Create**.

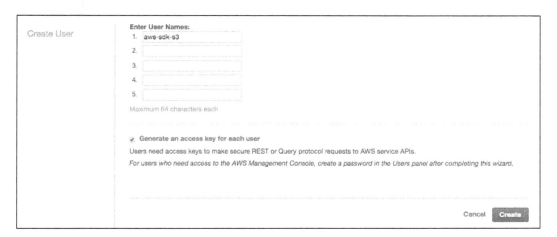

4. Click on **Download Credentials** and save the credentials. We will use the credentials composed of Access Key ID and Secret Access Key to access the S3 bucket.

5. Select the IAM user.

6. Click on **Attach User Policy**.

7. Click on **Select Policy Template** and then click on **Amazon S3 Full Access**.

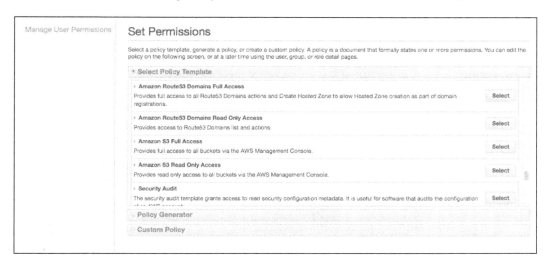

8. Click on **Apply Policy**.

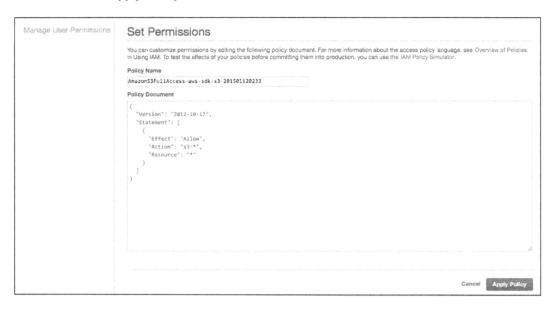

Next, we clone a repository for the S3 Java sample application and run the application by using the Maven command (mvn). First, we set up the AWS credentials to operate S3, clone the sample application repository from GitHub, and then build and run the sample application using the mvn command:

1. Create a credential file and put the access key ID and the secret access key in the credentials. You can see the access key ID and the secret access key in the credentials when we create an IAM user and retrieve the CSV file in the management console:

```
$ vim ~/.aws/credentials
[default]
aws_access_key_id = <YOUR_ACCESS_KEY_ID>
aws_secret_access_key = <YOUR_SECRET_ACCESS_KEY>
```

Downloading the example code

You can download the example code files from your account at
http://www.packtpub.com for all the Packt Publishing books
you have purchased. If you purchased this book elsewhere, you can
visit http://www.packtpub.com/support and register to
have the files e-mailed directly to you.

2. Download the sample SDK application:

```
$ git clone https://github.com/awslabs/aws-java-sample.git
$ cd aws-java-sample/
```

3. Run the sample application:

```
$ mvn clean compile exec:java
```

How it works...

The sample code works as shown in the following diagram; initiating the credentials to allow access Amazon S3, creating and listing a bucket in a region, putting, getting, and listing objects into the bucket, and then finally deleting the objects, and then the bucket:

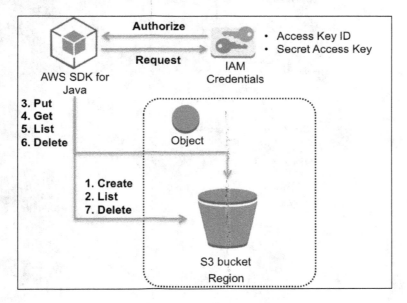

Now, let's run the sample application and see the output of the preceding command, as shown in the following screenshot, and then follow the source code step by step:

```
[ec2-user@ip-172-30-1-228 aws-java-sample]$ mvn clean compile exec:java
[INFO] Scanning for projects...
[INFO]
[INFO] ------------------------------------------------------------------------
[INFO] Building aws-java-sample 1.0
[INFO] ------------------------------------------------------------------------
[INFO]
[INFO] --- maven-clean-plugin:2.5:clean (default-clean) @ aws-java-sample ---
[INFO] Deleting /home/ec2-user/aws-java-sample/target
[INFO]
[INFO] --- maven-resources-plugin:2.6:resources (default-resources) @ aws-java-sample ---
[INFO] Using 'UTF-8' encoding to copy filtered resources.
[INFO] Copying 2 resources
[INFO]
[INFO] --- maven-compiler-plugin:3.1:compile (default-compile) @ aws-java-sample ---
[INFO] Changes detected - recompiling the module!
[INFO] Compiling 1 source file to /home/ec2-user/aws-java-sample/target/classes
[INFO]
[INFO] >>> exec-maven-plugin:1.2.1:java (default-cli) > validate @ aws-java-sample >>>
[INFO]
[INFO] <<< exec-maven-plugin:1.2.1:java (default-cli) < validate @ aws-java-sample <<<
[INFO]
[INFO] --- exec-maven-plugin:1.2.1:java (default-cli) @ aws-java-sample ---
===========================================
Getting Started with Amazon S3
===========================================

Creating bucket my-first-s3-bucket-07de44df-cce0-4089-a839-785b1a3c79ef

Listing buckets
 - my-first-s3-bucket-07de44df-cce0-4089-a839-785b1a3c79ef

Uploading a new object to S3 from a file

Downloading an object
Content-Type: text/plain
    abcdefghijklmnopqrstuvwxyz
    01234567890112345678901234
    !@#$%^&*()-=[]{};':',.<>/?
    01234567890112345678901234
    abcdefghijklmnopqrstuvwxyz

Listing objects
 - MyObjectKey  (size = 135)

Deleting an object

Deleting bucket my-first-s3-bucket-07de44df-cce0-4089-a839-785b1a3c79ef

[INFO] ------------------------------------------------------------------------
[INFO] BUILD SUCCESS
[INFO] ------------------------------------------------------------------------
[INFO] Total time: 8.229 s
[INFO] Finished at: 2015-07-08T01:07:32+00:00
[INFO] Final Memory: 16M/40M
[INFO] ------------------------------------------------------------------------
[ec2-user@ip-172-30-1-228 aws-java-sample]$
```

Then, let's examine the sample code at `aws-java-sample/src/main/java/com/amazonaws/samples/S3Sample.java`.

The `AmazonS3Client` method instantiates an AWS service client with the default credential provider chain (`~/.aws/credentials`). Then, the `Region.getRegion` method retrieves a region object, and chooses the US West (Oregon) region for the AWS client:

```
AmazonS3 s3 = new AmazonS3Client();
Region usWest2 = Region.getRegion(Regions.US_WEST_2);
s3.setRegion(usWest2);
```

 Amazon S3 creates a bucket in a region you specify and is available in several regions. For more information about S3 regions, refer to `http://docs.aws.amazon.com/general/latest/gr/rande.html#s3_region`.

The `createBucket` method creates an S3 bucket with the specified name in the specified region:

```
s3.createBucket(bucketName);
```

The `listBuckets` method lists and gets the bucket name:

```
for (Bucket bucket : s3.listBuckets()) {
System.out.println(" - " + bucket.getName());
```

The `putObject` method uploads objects into the specified bucket. The objects consist of the following code:

```
s3.putObject(new PutObjectRequest(bucketName, key,
createSampleFile()));
```

The `getObject` method gets the object stored in the specified bucket:

```
S3Object object = s3.getObject(new GetObjectRequest(bucketName,
key));
```

The `ListObjects` method returns a list of summary information of the object in the specified bucket:

```
ObjectListing objectListing = s3.listObjects(new
ListObjectsRequest()
```

The `deleteObject` method deletes the specified object in the specified bucket.

The reason to clean up objects before deleting the S3 bucket is that, it is unable to remove an S3 bucket with objects. We need to remove all objects in an S3 bucket first and then delete the bucket:

```
s3.deleteObject(bucketName, key);
```

The `deleteBucket` method deletes the specified bucket in the region.

The `AmazonServiceException` class provides the error messages, for example, the request ID, HTTP status code, the AWS error code, for a failed request from the client in order to examine the request. On the other hand, the `AmazonClientException` class can be used for mainly providing error responses when the client is unable to get a response from AWS resources or successfully make the service call, for example, a client failed to make a service call because no network was present:

```
s3.deleteBucket(bucketName);
} catch (AmazonServiceException ase) {
    System.out.println("Caught an AmazonServiceException, which
    means your request made it " + "to Amazon S3, but was rejected
    with an error response for some reason.");
    System.out.println("Error Message:    " + ase.getMessage());
    System.out.println("HTTP Status Code:    " + ase.getStatusCode());
    System.out.println("AWS Error Code:    " + ase.getErrorCode());
    System.out.println("Error Type:    " + ase.getErrorType());
    System.out.println("Request ID:    " + ase.getRequestId());
    } catch (AmazonClientException ace) {
        System.out.println("Caught an AmazonClientException, which
        means the client encountered " + "a serious internal problem
        while trying to communicate with S3," + "such as not being
        able to access the network.");
        System.out.println("Error Message: " + ace.getMessage());
```

See also

► AWS SDK for the Java sample application, available at `https://github.com/aws/aws-sdk-java`

► Developer Guide available at `http://docs.aws.amazon.com/AWSSdkDocsJava/latest/DeveloperGuide/`

► The API documentation available at `http://docs.aws.amazon.com/AWSJavaSDK/latest/javadoc/`

► Creating the IAM user in your AWS account, available at `http://docs.aws.amazon.com/IAM/latest/UserGuide/Using_SettingUpUser.html`

Learning AWS SDK for Node.js and basic S3 operations with sample code

This section introduces you about how to install AWS SDK for Node.js and how to create S3 buckets, put objects, get objects using the sample code, and explains how the sample code runs as well.

Getting ready

AWS SDK for JavaScript is available for browsers and mobile services, on the other hand Node.js supports as backend. Each API call is exposed as a function on the service.

To get started with AWS SDK for Node.js, it is necessary to install the following on your development machine:

- Node.js (http://nodejs.org/)
- npm (https://www.npmjs.com/package/npm)

How to do it...

Proceed with the following steps to install the packages and run the sample application. The preferred way to install SDK is to use npm, the package manager for Node.js.

1. Download the sample SDK application:

   ```
   $ git clone https://github.com/awslabs/aws-nodejs-sample.git
   $ cd aws-nodejs-sample/
   ```

2. Run the sample application:

   ```
   $ node sample.js
   ```

How it works...

The sample code works as shown in the following diagram; initiating the credentials to allow access to Amazon S3, creating a bucket in a region, putting objects into the bucket, and then, finally, deleting the objects and the bucket. Make sure that you delete the objects and the bucket yourself after running this sample application because the application does not delete the bucket:

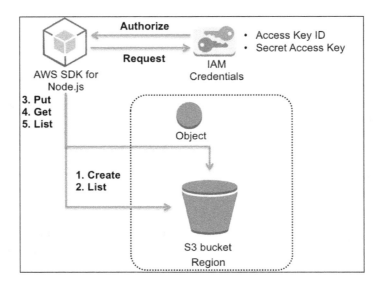

Now, let's run the sample application and see the output of the command, as shown in the following screenshot, and then follow the source code step by step:

```
[ec2-user@ip-172-30-1-228 aws-nodejs-sample]$ node sample.js
Successfully uploaded data to node-sdk-sample-8483f463-a2ca-46ae-bc2a-9c0b6ab98204/hello_world.txt
[ec2-user@ip-172-30-1-228 aws-nodejs-sample]$
```

Now, let's examine the sample code; the path is aws-nodejs-sample/sample.js. The AWS.S3 method creates an AWS client:

```
var s3 = new AWS.S3();
```

The createBucket method creates an S3 bucket with the specified name defined as the bucketName variable. The bucket is created in the standard US region, by default. The putObject method uploads an object defined as the keyName variable into the bucket:

```
var bucketName = 'node-sdk-sample-' + uuid.v4();
var keyName = 'hello_world.txt';
```

```
s3.createBucket({Bucket: bucketName}, function() {
  var params = {Bucket: bucketName, Key: keyName, Body: 'Hello
  World!'};
  s3.putObject(params, function(err, data) {
    if (err)
      console.log(err)
    else
      console.log("Successfully uploaded data to " + bucketName +
      "/" + keyName);
  });
});
```

The whole sample code is as follows:

```
var AWS = require('aws-sdk');
var uuid = require('node-uuid');
var s3 = new AWS.S3();
var bucketName = 'node-sdk-sample-' + uuid.v4();
var keyName = 'hello_world.txt';
s3.createBucket({Bucket: bucketName}, function() {
  var params = {Bucket: bucketName, Key: keyName, Body: 'Hello
  World!'};
  s3.putObject(params, function(err, data) {
    if (err)
      console.log(err)
    else
      console.log("Successfully uploaded data to " + bucketName +
      "/" + keyName);
  });
});
```

See also

▶ AWS SDK for the Node.js sample application, available at
   `https://github.com/aws/aws-sdk-js`

▶ Developer Guide available at `http://docs.aws.amazon.com/`
   `AWSJavaScriptSDK/guide/index.html`

▶ The API documentation available at `http://docs.aws.amazon.com/`
   `AWSJavaScriptSDK/latest/index.html`

Learning AWS SDK for Python and basic S3 operations with sample code

This section introduces you about how to install AWS SDK for Python and how to create S3 buckets, put objects, get objects using the sample code, and explains how the sample code runs as well.

Getting ready

Boto, a Python interface, is offered by Amazon Web Services and all of its features work with Python 2.6 and 2.7. The next major version to support Python 3.3 is underway.

To get started with AWS SDK for Python (Boto), it is necessary to install the following on your development machine:

- Python (`https://www.python.org/`)
- pip (`http://pip.readthedocs.org/en/latest/index.html`)
- Boto (`https://github.com/boto/boto`)

How to do it...

Proceed with the following steps to install the packages and run the sample application:

1. Download the sample SDK application:

    ```
    $ git clone https://github.com/awslabs/aws-python-sample.git
    $ cd aws-python-sample/
    ```

2. Run the sample application:

    ```
    $ python s3_sample.py
    ```

How it works...

The sample code works as shown in the following diagram; initiating the credentials to allow access to Amazon S3, creating a bucket in a region, putting and getting objects into the bucket, and then finally deleting the objects and the bucket.

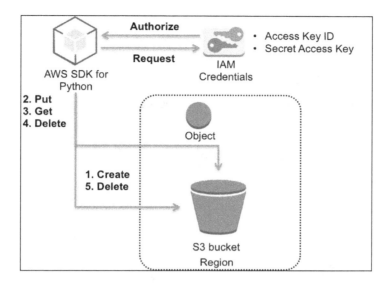

Now, let's run the sample application and see the output of the preceding command, as shown in the following screenshot, and then follow the source code step by step:

```
[ec2-user@ip-172-30-1-228 aws-python-sample]$ python s3_sample.py
Creating new bucket with name: python-sdk-sample-89809de8-cce6-41d7-973e-b622773f429d
Uploading some data to python-sdk-sample-89809de8-cce6-41d7-973e-b622773f429d with key: python_sample
_key.txt
Generating a public URL for the object we just uploaded. This URL will be active for 1800 seconds

https://python-sdk-sample-89809de8-cce6-41d7-973e-b622773f429d.s3.amazonaws.com/python_sample_key.txt
?Signature=tkNS9Chzx7lCIy3AGrg1nYA99hs%3D&Expires=1436324298&AWSAccessKeyId=AKIAIILAY4IR4IKXF22A

Press enter to delete both the object and the bucket...
Deleting the object.
Deleting the bucket.
[ec2-user@ip-172-30-1-228 aws-python-sample]$
```

Now, let's examine the sample code; the path is `aws-python-sample/s3-sample.py`.

The `connect_s3` method creates a connection for accessing S3:

```
s3 = boto.connect_s3()
```

The `create_bucket` method creates an S3 bucket with the specified name defined as the `bucket_name` variable in the standard US region by default:

```
bucket_name = "python-sdk-sample-%s" % uuid.uuid4()
print "Creating new bucket with name: " + bucket_name
bucket = s3.create_bucket(bucket_name)
```

By creating a new `key` object, it stores new data in the bucket:

```
from boto.s3.key import Key
k = Key(bucket)
k.key = 'python_sample_key.txt'
```

The `delete` method deletes all the objects in the bucket:

```
k.delete()
```

The `delete_bucket` method deletes the bucket:

```
bucket.s3.delete_bucket(bucket_name)
```

The whole sample code is as follows:

```
import boto
import uuid
s3 = boto.connect_s3()
bucket_name = "python-sdk-sample-%s" % uuid.uuid4()
print "Creating new bucket with name: " + bucket_name
bucket = s3.create_bucket(bucket_name)
from boto.s3.key import Key
k = Key(bucket)
k.key = 'python_sample_key.txt'
print "Uploading some data to " + bucket_name + " with key: " +
k.key
k.set_contents_from_string('Hello World!')
expires_in_seconds = 1800
print "Generating a public URL for the object we just uploaded.
This URL will be active for %d seconds" % expires_in_seconds
print
print k.generate_url(expires_in_seconds)
print
raw_input("Press enter to delete both the object and the
bucket...")
print "Deleting the object."
k.delete()
print "Deleting the bucket."
s3.delete_bucket(bucket_name)
```

See also

▸ AWS SDK for the Python sample application, available at
`https://github.com/boto/boto`

▸ Developer Guide and the API documentation available at
`http://boto.readthedocs.org/en/latest/`

Learning AWS SDK for Ruby and basic S3 operations with sample code

This section introduces you about how to install AWS SDK for Ruby and how to create S3 buckets, put objects, get objects using the sample code, and explains how the sample code runs as well.

Getting ready

The AWS SDK for Ruby provides a Ruby API operation and enables developer help complicated coding by providing Ruby classes. New users should start with AWS SDK for Ruby V2, as officially recommended.

To get started with AWS SDK for Ruby, it is necessary to install the following on your development machine:

▸ Ruby (`https://www.ruby-lang.org/`)

▸ Bundler (`http://bundler.io/`)

How to do it...

Proceed with the following steps to install the packages and run the sample application. We install the stable AWS SDK for Ruby v2 and download the sample code.

1. Download the sample SDK application:

```
$ git clone https://github.com/awslabs/aws-ruby-sample.git
$ cd aws-ruby-sample/
```

2. Run the sample application:

```
$ bundle install
$ ruby s3_sample.rb
```

How it works...

The sample code works as shown in the following diagram; initiating the credentials to allow access to Amazon S3, creating a bucket in a region, putting and getting objects into the bucket, and then finally deleting the objects and the bucket.

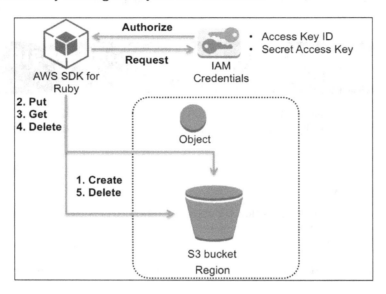

Now, let's run the sample application and see the output of the preceding command, which is shown in the following screenshot, and then follow the source code step by step:

```
[ec2-user@ip-172-30-1-228 aws-ruby-sample]$ ruby s3_sample.rb
[WARNING] MultiJson is using the default adapter (ok_json).We recommend loading a different JSON library to impro
ve performance.
Created an object in S3 at:
https://ruby-sdk-sample-ce326ab0-074a-0133-2756-063549312906.s3-us-west-2.amazonaws.com/ruby_sample_key.txt

Use this URL to download the file:
https://ruby-sdk-sample-ce326ab0-074a-0133-2756-063549312906.s3-us-west-2.amazonaws.com/ruby_sample_key.txt?X-Amz
-Algorithm=AWS4-HMAC-SHA256&X-Amz-Credential=AKIAIILAY4IR4IKXF22A%2F20150708%2Fus-west-2%2Fs3%2Faws4_request&X-Am
z-Date=20150708T025609Z&X-Amz-Expires=900&X-Amz-SignedHeaders=host&X-Amz-Signature=7374d551e9a50bd06010bd6ad8b130
11268b990889b9d05ce10ac3e90f64546b
(press any key to delete both the bucket and the object)

Deleting bucket ruby-sdk-sample-ce326ab0-074a-0133-2756-063549312906
[ec2-user@ip-172-30-1-228 aws-ruby-sample]$
```

Now, let's examine the sample code; the path is `aws-ruby-sample/s3-sample.rb`.

The `AWS::S3.new` method creates an AWS client:

```
s3 = AWS::S3.new
```

The `s3.buckets.create` method creates an S3 bucket with the specified name defined as the `bucket_name` variable in the standard US region by default:

```
uuid = UUID.new
bucket_name = "ruby-sdk-sample-#{uuid.generate}"
bucket = s3.bucket(bucket_name)
bucket.create
```

The `objects.put` method puts an object defined as the `objects` variable in the bucket:

```
object = bucket.object('ruby_sample_key.txt')
object.put(body: "Hello World!")
```

The `object.public_url` method creates a public URL for the object:

```
puts object.public_url
```

The `object.url_for(:read)` method creates a public URL to read an object:

```
puts object.url_for(:read)
```

The `bucket.delete!` method deletes all the objects in a bucket, and then deletes the bucket:

```
bucket.delete!
```

The whole sample code is as follows:

```ruby
#!/usr/bin/env ruby
require 'rubygems'
require 'bundler/setup'
require 'aws-sdk'
require 'uuid'
s3 = Aws::S3::Resource.new(region: 'us-west-2')
uuid = UUID.new
bucket_name = "ruby-sdk-sample-#{uuid.generate}"
bucket = s3.bucket(bucket_name)
bucket.create
object = bucket.object('ruby_sample_key.txt')
object.put(body: "Hello World!")
puts "Created an object in S3 at:"
puts object.public_url
puts "\nUse this URL to download the file:"
puts object.presigned_url(:get)
puts "(press any key to delete both the bucket and the object)"
$stdin.getc
puts "Deleting bucket #{bucket_name}"
bucket.delete!
```

See also

▸ AWS SDK for the Ruby sample application, available at
   `https://github.com/aws/aws-sdk-ruby`

▸ Developer Guide available at `http://docs.aws.amazon.com/`
   `AWSSdkDocsRuby/latest/DeveloperGuide/`

▸ The API documentation available at `http://docs.aws.amazon.com/`
   `sdkforruby/api/frames.html`

Learning AWS SDK for PHP and basic S3 operations with sample code

This section introduces you about how to install AWS SDK for PHP and how to create S3 buckets, put objects, get objects using the sample code, and explains how the sample code runs as well.

Getting ready

AWS SDK for PHP is a powerful tool for PHP developers to quickly build their stable applications.

To get started with AWS SDK for PHP, it is necessary to install the following on your development machine:

▸ PHP-5.3.3+, compiled with the uCRL extension (`http://php.net/`)

▸ Composer (`https://getcomposer.org/`)

It is recommended to use Composer to install AWS SDK for PHP because it is much easier than getting the source code.

How to do it...

Proceed with the following steps to install the packages and run the sample application:

1. Download the sample SDK application:

   ```
   $ git clone https://github.com/awslabs/aws-php-sample.git
   $ cd aws-php-sample/
   ```

2. Run the sample application:

   ```
   $ php sample.php
   ```

How it works...

The sample code works as shown in the following diagram; initiating the credentials to allow access to Amazon S3, creating a bucket in a region, putting and getting objects into the bucket, and then finally deleting the objects and the bucket:

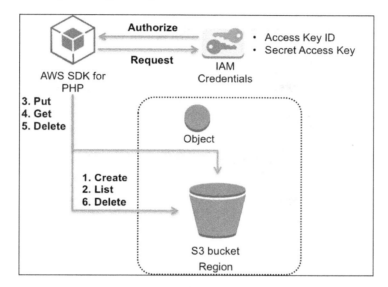

Now, let's run the sample application and see the output of the preceding command, as shown in the following screenshot, and then follow the source code step by step:

```
[ec2-user@ip-172-30-1-228 aws-php-sample]$ php sample.php
Creating bucket named php-sdk-sample-54b323ca6aab22.73347302
Creating a new object with key hello_world.txt
Downloading that same object:

---BEGIN---
Hello World!
---END---

Deleting object with key hello_world.txt
Deleting bucket php-sdk-sample-54b323ca6aab22.73347302
```

Now, let's examine the sample code; the path is `aws-php-sample/sample.php`.

The `s3Client::facory` method creates an AWS client and is the easiest way to get up and running:

```
$client = S3Client::factory();
```

The `createBucket` method creates an S3 bucket with the specified name in a region defined in the credentials file:

```
$result = $client->createBucket(array(
    'Bucket' => $bucket
));
```

The `PutOjbect` method uploads objects into the bucket:

```
$key = 'hello_world.txt';
$result = $client->putObject(array(
    'Bucket' => $bucket,
    'Key'    => $key,
    'Body'   => "Hello World!"
));
```

The `getObject` method retrieves objects from the bucket:

```
$result = $client->getObject(array(
    'Bucket' => $bucket,
    'Key'    => $key
));
```

The `deleteObject` method removes objects from the bucket:

```
$result = $client->deleteObject(array(
    'Bucket' => $bucket,
    'Key'    => $key
));
```

The `deleteBucket` method deletes the bucket:

```
$result = $client->deleteBucket(array(
    'Bucket' => $bucket
));
```

The whole sample code is as follows:

```
<?php
use Aws\S3\S3Client;
$client = S3Client::factory();
$bucket = uniqid("php-sdk-sample-", true);
echo "Creating bucket named {$bucket}\n";
$result = $client->createBucket(array(
    'Bucket' => $bucket
));
```

```php
$client->waitUntilBucketExists(array('Bucket' => $bucket));
$key = 'hello_world.txt';
echo "Creating a new object with key {$key}\n";
$result = $client->putObject(array(
    'Bucket' => $bucket,
    'Key'    => $key,
    'Body'   => "Hello World!"
));
echo "Downloading that same object:\n";
$result = $client->getObject(array(
    'Bucket' => $bucket,
    'Key'    => $key
));
echo "\n---BEGIN---\n";
echo $result['Body'];
echo "\n---END---\n\n";
echo "Deleting object with key {$key}\n";
$result = $client->deleteObject(array(
    'Bucket' => $bucket,
    'Key'    => $key
));
echo "Deleting bucket {$bucket}\n";
$result = $client->deleteBucket(array(
    'Bucket' => $bucket
));
```

See also

- AWS SDK for the PHP sample application,. available at
  https://github.com/aws/aws-sdk-php

- Developer Guide available at
  http://docs.aws.amazon.com/aws-sdk-php/guide/latest/index.html

- The API documentation available at
  http://docs.aws.amazon.com/aws-sdk-php/latest/

2

Hosting a Static Website on Amazon S3 Bucket

Instead of running Web servers such as Apache or Nginx on EC2 instances, Amazon S3 supports hosting a static website content over Amazon S3 buckets. It is much easier rather than installing, running, and managing your web servers on your own because all you need to do is to create a bucket, add a website configuration to your bucket, apply a bucket policy, and upload your contents, plus configure a custom domain if you want to use your own domain.

In this chapter, you will learn how to:

- ▶ How to configure a static website on Amazon S3 bucket
- ▶ How to configure S3 server access logging
- ▶ How to configure a static website using a custom domain
- ▶ How to configure a static website on Amazon S3 bucket with AWS CLI

Introduction

Amazon S3 is not only storing objects on buckets and accessing them over the Internet, but is also available as a static website with client-side techniques such as HTML, CSS, and JavaScript, which does not require server-side scripts such as ASP.NET, PHP, or JSP.

The benefits of hosting a static website on Amazon S3 are as follows:

▶ **Low cost**: The charges are data storing and data transfer fees

▶ **Reliable routing**: This allows you to map a custom domain and route customers to your website with Route53

▶ **Low latency**: This delivers the content from the closest location to the customer by caching the content in the edge location over the world with CloudFront

▶ **Low maintenance**: Amazon S3 consists of an automatic self-hearing infrastructure and is designed with 99.999999999 percent durability and 99.99 percent availability of objects over a given year by synchronously storing your data across multiple facilities

How to configure a static website on Amazon S3 bucket

In this section, we will create an S3 bucket and enable website hosting configuring properties and adding a bucket policy on the bucket through the S3 console. Next, we will upload a sample static content to the bucket, and verify that the content is available over the Internet in the browser.

Getting ready

You don't need to request or fill-in any form to host a static website on Amazon S3 through the Amazon Management Console; nor do you pay any initial cost.

Before configuring a static website on Amazon S3, all you need to do is sign up to the AWS management console and access S3 using your IAM credentials.

How to do it...

Proceed with the following steps to host a static website on the Amazon S3 bucket. The point is to apply a bucket policy and enable a static website over the bucket after creating an S3 bucket and uploading your content through the S3 management console. Finally, an S3 website endpoint is generated, and you can access your content through the website endpoint.

1. Sign in to the AWS management console and move to the S3 console available at `https://console.aws.amazon.com/s3`.

2. You will see a **Create Bucket** button on the screen. Just click on it.

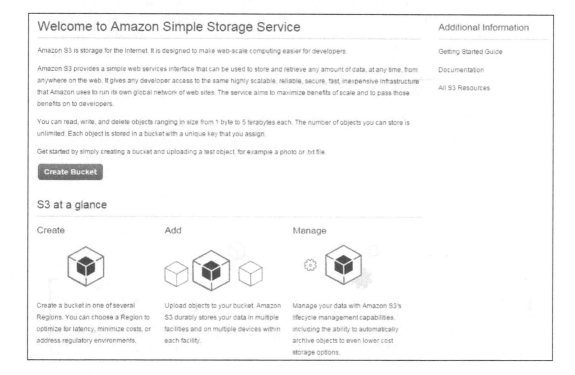

 Check storage, request and data transfer pricing before creating a bucket because they differ in regions: `http://aws.amazon.com/s3/pricing/`.

3. You will then get a dialog box in which you need to fill in some details. In the dialog box, input a name for your bucket in the **Bucket Name** field, choose the region you want in the **Region** field, and click on **Create**.

I recommend that you choose the US Standard or the US West (Oregon) region because they are the cheapest in storage, request, and data transfer pricing. However, if you care about latency, you should choose the closest region from your location.

See Bucket Restrictions and Limitations for bucket naming guidelines at `http://docs.aws.amazon.com/AmazonS3/latest/dev/BucketRestrictions.html`.

You can enable Server Access Logging when creating a bucket. However, we will skip setting up Server Access Logging and enable it later.

4. As shown in the following screenshot, click on the name of the bucket, and then click on **Properties**:

5. Click on **Static Website Hosting** and then select **Enable website hosting**. Refer to the following screenshot for more clarification:

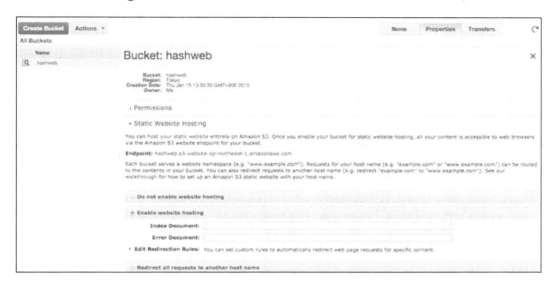

6. As shown in the following screenshot, add the name of your index document in the **Index Document** section, and click on **Save**.

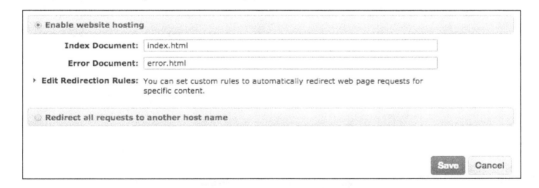

Amazon S3 supports index documents. If a user visits `http://example.com` on the browser, Amazon S3 returns the index document path and a webpage is returned to the root of a website or any subfolder. For more information, refer to the URL `http://docs.aws.amazon.com/AmazonS3/latest/dev/IndexDocumentSupport.html`.

On the other hand, an error document is optional. If you specify the error document and a user requests a webpage that doesn't exist, Amazon S3 returns the webpage defined in the error document with a 404 HTTP response code.

7. Then write down the website endpoint at **Endpoint**.

▾ Static Website Hosting

You can host your static website entirely on Amazon S3. Once you enable your bucket for static website hosting, all your content is accessible to web browsers via the Amazon S3 website endpoint for your bucket.

Endpoint: hashweb.s3-website-ap-northeast-1.amazonaws.com

Each bucket serves a website namespace (e.g. "www.example.com"). Requests for your host name (e.g. "example.com" or "www.example.com") can be routed to the contents in your bucket. You can also redirect requests to another host name (e.g. redirect "example.com" to "www.example.com"). See our walkthrough for how to set up an Amazon S3 static website with your host name.

The Amazon S3 endpoint is region-specific. For example, when you choose the US West (Oregon) region for your bucket, the endpoint for the static website should be `<your_bucket>.s3-website-us-west-2.amazonaws.com` and you can see the website at `http://<your_bucket>.s3-website-us-west-2.amazonaws.com/`.

You can check the entire region and endpoints in the Amazon Simple Storage Service Website Endpoints section at `http://docs.aws.amazon.com/general/latest/gr/rande.html#s3_region`.

8. Select **Permissions** and click on **Add bucket policy** to make the bucket content publicly available. These settings are marked in the following screenshot:

9. Copy the bucket policy below and paste it in **Bucket Policy Editor**. Replace `<your_bucket>` with your bucket name in the policy. The meaning of the elements in the bucket policy is as follows:

    ❑ `Sid`: The statement Id (Sid) is an identifier for the policy statement.

    ❑ `Effect`: This can be `Allow` or `Deny`. `Allow` effects when the user requests for a specific action; the action can be allowed.

    ❑ `Principal`: This defines which account or user is allowed to access the actions and resources. An asterisk (*) allows any user to access the actions and resources.

    ❑ `Action`: This defines a set of resource operations; for example, getting objects, putting objects, and so on.

    ❑ `Resource`: This defines the buckets and objects to be allowed or denied access. The **Amazon Resource Name** (**ARN**) is used to identify the resources.

 For more about bucket policy language, refer to the URL `http://docs.aws.amazon.com/AmazonS3/latest/dev/access-policy-language-overview.html`.
Amazon S3 permissions for object operations can be found at `http://docs.aws.amazon.com/AmazonS3/latest/dev/using-with-s3-actions.html`.

The following code snippet is the bucket policy we used:

```
{
"Version":"2012-10-17",
"Statement":[{
"Sid":"PublicReadGetObjects",
"Effect":"Allow",
"Principal": "*",
"Action":["s3:GetObject"],
"Resource":["arn:aws:s3:::<your_bucket>/*"]
}]
}
```

The following screenshot shows the bucket policy editor:

 Before applying the bucket policy to a bucket, 403 Forbidden replies and the access is denied.

10. In the bucket list, click on the name of the bucket and then click on **Upload**.

11. Drag and drop the files and folders to upload and click on **Start Upload**. Refer to the screenshot for better understanding:

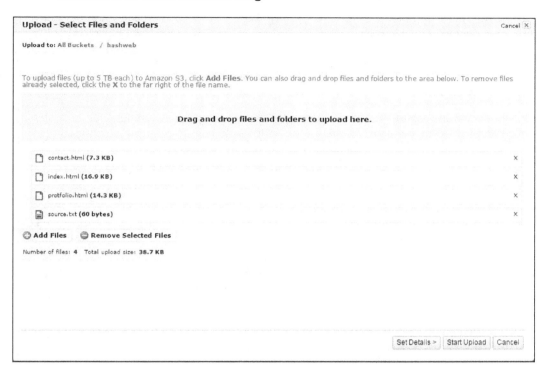

12. After the upload is successful, it shows **Done** as shown in the following screenshot:

How it works...

Type the endpoint in the browser and test your website so that you can see your contents through Amazon S3 as a static website.

When an S3 static website is configured, an Amazon S3 website endpoint is automatically generated for the bucket. It is called Website Endpoints and the website endpoints do not support HTTPS, only HTTP.

As the website endpoints are bucket names and region-specific, you cannot change or specify the endpoint, but you can use CNAME for the endpoint to access with your custom domain such as `http://www.yourdomain.com/`.

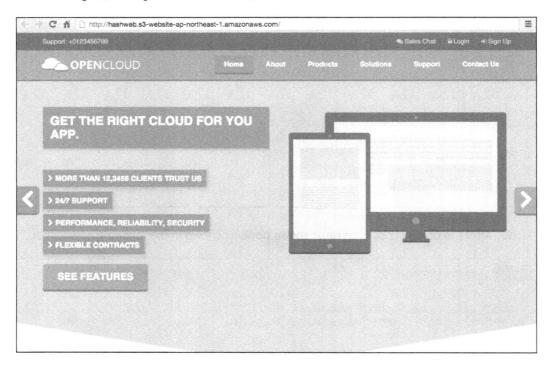

After configuring a static website over the bucket, you can see that the endpoint uses the CNAME record, looking up the S3 website endpoint with the `dig` command, as follows:

```
$ dig hashweb.s3-website-ap-northeast-1.amazonaws.com

; <<>>DiG 9.8.3-P1 <<>> hashweb.s3-website-ap-northeast-
1.amazonaws.com
;; global options: +cmd
;; Got answer:
```

```
;; ->>HEADER<<- opcode: QUERY, status: NOERROR, id: 45068
;; flags: qrrdra; QUERY: 1, ANSWER: 2, AUTHORITY: 4, ADDITIONAL: 4

;; QUESTION SECTION:
;hashweb.s3-website-ap-northeast-1.amazonaws.com. IN A

;; ANSWER SECTION:
hashweb.s3-website-ap-northeast-1.amazonaws.com. 60 IN CNAME s3-
website-ap-northeast-1.amazonaws.com.
s3-website-ap-northeast-1.amazonaws.com. 31 IN A 54.231.226.19
```

If you configure your error document in the **Error Document** section and type a path that doesn't exist, you can see that the error document appears:

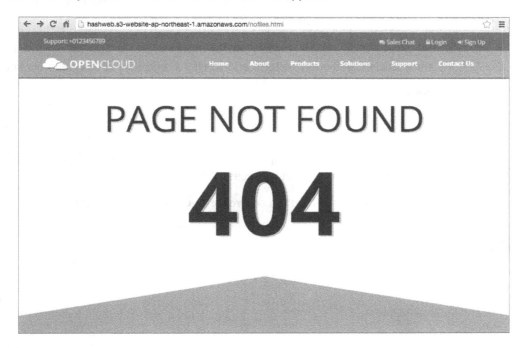

See also

- ▸ Hosting a Static Website on Amazon S3 available at `http://docs.aws.amazon.com/AmazonS3/latest/dev/WebsiteHosting.html`
- ▸ Website Endpoint, available at `http://docs.aws.amazon.com/AmazonS3/latest/dev/WebsiteEndpoints.html`
- ▸ Custom Error Document Support, available at `http://docs.aws.amazon.com/AmazonS3/latest/dev/CustomErrorDocSupport.html`

How to configure S3 server access logging

This section describes about how to record access logging for access to your bucket because S3 server access logging is disabled, by default, and S3 does not store server access in the log files. We will configure server access logging over an S3 bucket and verify that log files are generated when we access the S3 website.

Getting ready

If you run a web server, you may want to see and analyze the web server's access log files for the access to your website. To configure server access logging, you need to enable S3 Server Access Logging for your bucket on your own because it is not enabled by default. You can choose two ways to store access log objects in an S3 bucket, as follows:

1. Create another bucket for server access logging.
2. Use the same bucket for a static website and specify a target prefix under the bucket.

We will be using the same bucket for logging by specifying a target prefix.

How to do it...

It is simple to enable S3 Server Access logging. All you have to do is enable the function, and specify the bucket and the target prefix to store access log objects.

1. Click on the name of the bucket, then on **Properties**, and finally on **Logging**:

2. In the **Logging** section, select **Enabled,** and select the bucket in **Target Bucket**. Specify a value in the **Target Prefix** field, and click on **Save** as shown in the following screenshot:

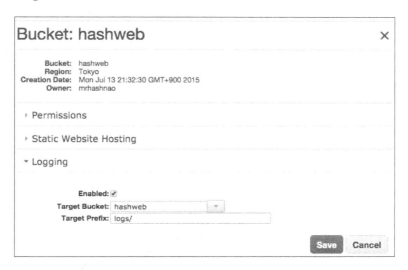

3. Select **Permissions**, and confirm whether a **Grantee** called `Log Delivery` is added with the following permissions:

How it works...

After a couple of minutes, you can see that the log objects have been stored in the target prefix as below. For example, if you specify the target prefix `logs/`, the log objects are stored at `<target_bucket>/logs/`.

Name	Storage Class	Size	Last Modified
2015-01-17-11-16-43-F1533C4FB0E7B619	Standard	608 bytes	Sat Jan 17 20:16:44 GMT+900 2015
2015-01-17-11-19-08-667BA4F9E88609DF	Standard	279 bytes	Sat Jan 17 20:19:10 GMT+900 2015
2015-01-17-11-22-52-1F2760711AD9A272	Standard	8.5 KB	Sat Jan 17 20:22:53 GMT+900 2015
2015-01-17-11-26-08-9AB58772DE7B41EE	Standard	1.2 KB	Sat Jan 17 20:26:10 GMT+900 2015
2015-01-17-11-27-23-B149C91396BBFFB9	Standard	13.4 KB	Sat Jan 17 20:27:24 GMT+900 2015
2015-01-17-12-17-58-9D3F20593E71FE28	Standard	1.4 KB	Sat Jan 17 21:17:59 GMT+900 2015
2015-01-17-12-18-01-35151BA1A433103D	Standard	4.7 KB	Sat Jan 17 21:18:02 GMT+900 2015
2015-01-17-12-19-11-56BE22007750C279	Standard	2.6 KB	Sat Jan 17 21:19:12 GMT+900 2015
2015-01-17-12-20-45-621998BB08A2B120	Standard	1.4 KB	Sat Jan 17 21:20:46 GMT+900 2015

After you access your website on an S3 bucket, you can open a log file and see the access as follows:

```
e402e5b35ef20f6f3eeba038ec5bc4d76c2b88e2ba3bcca29f5e8e6aeab91a3aha
shweb [17/Jan/2015:11:00:58 +0000] xxx.xxx.xxx.xxx -
47CDB1149A64388E WEBSITE.GET.OBJECT js/jquery-1.10.2.min.js "GET
/js/jquery-1.10.2.min.js HTTP/1.1" 304 - - 93107 18 -
"http://hashweb.s3-website-ap-northeast-
1.amazonaws.com/index.html" "Mozilla/5.0 (Macintosh; Intel Mac OS
X 10_10_1) AppleWebKit/537.36 (KHTML, like Gecko)
Chrome/39.0.2171.95 Safari/537.36" -
```

 For S3 Server Access Logging Format, refer to the URL `http://docs.aws.amazon.com/AmazonS3/latest/dev/LogFormat.html`.

There's more...

Now, let's discuss the S3 Server Access Log Object Key Format.

The log object key format is `<target_prefix>YYYY-mm-DD-HH-MM-SS-UniqueString`.

In the key string, `YYYY`, `mm`, `DD`, `HH`, `MM`, and `SS` are the digits of the year, month, day, hour, minute, and seconds when the log object was delivered. `UniqueString` prevents overwriting the log object and has a special meaning.

The basic rules of S3 Server Access Logging pricing are follows:

- No extra charge for enabling S3 Server Access Logging
- No charge for data transfer for log delivery
- Storing log objects is charged in the same way as S3 storage pricing
- Access to the log objects is charged in the same way as S3 data transfer pricing

 The point is that log objects keep increasing and storage charge costs also increase, by default, as they grow. If you want to regularly delete log objects, you can manage the life cycle of objects by using life cycle rules. We will discuss this topic in *Chapter 9, Enabling Cross-origin Resource Sharing*.

See also

- Server Access Logging, available at `http://docs.aws.amazon.com/AmazonS3/latest/dev/ServerLogs.html`
- Server Access Log Format, available at `http://docs.aws.amazon.com/AmazonS3/latest/dev/LogFormat.html`

How to configure a static website using a custom domain

In the *How to configure a static website on Amazon S3 bucket* recipe, we created a static website on Amazon S3 bucket and we can access the website through a website endpoint. However, most of the customers want to use your custom domain for your website such as `http://<your-blog-site>.com/` or `http://www.<your-blog-site>.com/`. In order to use a custom domain, we need to create two S3 buckets, configure a website redirect, and use Route 53 for creating a DNS record.

Getting ready

We hosted a static website on Amazon S3. Then, let's configure a static website using your custom domain.

We use two buckets to allow access for both `http://www.<your_domain>/` and `http://<your_domain>` by redirecting from `www.<your_domain>` to `<your_domain>`.

Regarding redirect, this section describes from `www.hashnao.info` to `hashnao.info`.

Make sure that you meet the following requirements:

► Request and register your domain name for the website

► Sign up on AWS and access to S3 and Route53 with your IAM credentials

► Create a bucket named `<your_domain>`, upload your contents into the bucket, apply a bucket policy to the bucket, enable website hosting by following the instruction given in *How to configure a static website on Amazon S3 bucket*

► Create a bucket named `www.<your_domain>`

How to do it...

First, we create and configure a Hosted Zone in the Amazon Route 53 console, add an Alias record, and enable redirect to the bucket named www.<your_domain> in the Amazon S3 console.

1. Sign in to the AWS management console and move to the Route53 console at `https://console.aws.amazon.com/route53/home`.

2. Click on **Hosted Zones** and create a **Hosted Zone**.

3. In the **Domain Name** box, enter `<your_domain>`, select **Public Hosted Zone** in the **Type** box, and click on **Create** as shown in the following screenshot:

4. Select the domain and click on **Go to Record Set** and write down the Amazon Route 53 **name servers** (**NS**) for this domain.

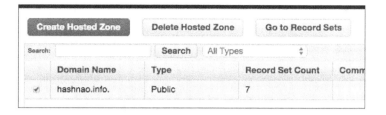

5. Go to your DNS provider site and update the name server (NS) record.

 For more information about how to update the NS record, refer to the URL http://docs.aws.amazon.com/Route53/latest/DeveloperGuide/MigratingDNS.html#Step_UpdateRegistrar.

6. Click on **Create Record Set** and select **A – Ipv4 address** in the **Type** box, **Yes** in the **Alias** box, <your_domain> bucket name in the **Alias Target** box, and click on **Save Record Set**.

7. Create another A record for `www.<your_domain>` in the same way.

8. Confirm both the A records are registered using the `dig` or `host` commands:

    ```
    $ dig www.hashnao.info A


    ; <<>> DiG 9.8.3-P1 <<>> www.hashnao.info A
    ;; global options: +cmd
    ;; Got answer:
    ;; ->>HEADER<<- opcode: QUERY, status: NOERROR, id: 59203
    ;; flags: qr rd ra; QUERY: 1, ANSWER: 1, AUTHORITY: 0,
    ADDITIONAL: 0


    ;; QUESTION SECTION:
    ;www.hashnao.info.      IN   A


    ;; ANSWER SECTION:
    www.hashnao.info.  60  IN  A  54.231.229.12


    $ dig hashnao.info A


    ; <<>> DiG 9.8.3-P1 <<>> hashnao.info A
    ;; global options: +cmd
    ;; Got answer:
    ;; ->>HEADER<<- opcode: QUERY, status: NOERROR, id: 4141
    ;; flags: qr rd ra; QUERY: 1, ANSWER: 1, AUTHORITY: 0,
    ADDITIONAL: 0


    ;; QUESTION SECTION:
    ;hashnao.info.       IN   A


    ;; ANSWER SECTION:
    hashnao.info.     60  IN  A  54.231.229.20
    ```

    We move to the Amazon S3 console and configure redirect over the bucket named `www.<your_domain>`.

9. Sign in to the AWS management console and move to the S3 console at `https://console.aws.amazon.com/s3`.

10. Click on the bucket named www.<your_domain>, then on **Properties**, and finally on **Static Website Hosting**; select **Redirect all requests to another hostname**.

In the **Redirect all request to** box, enter <your_domain> and click on **Save**.

How it works...

First, we confirm whether http://<your_domain> is available over the Internet, and then redirect from http://www.<your_domain>to http://<your_domain>.

1. Type http://<your_domain>/ in the browser and confirm whether your content is available.

2. Type http://www.<your_domain>/ in the browser and confirm whether it redirects to http://<your_domain>/.

See also

▶ Setting Up a Static Website Using a Custom Domain available at http://docs.aws.amazon.com/AmazonS3/latest/dev/website-hosting-custom-domain-walkthrough.html

How to configure a static website on Amazon S3 bucket with AWS CLI

We created or configured S3 buckets through the S3 management console so far. However, the problem is that it takes time if you do the same thing again and again. If you use AWS CLI, you don't need to sign in on the AWS management console and can finish your work with the command-line alone.

Getting ready

It is sometimes tiresome to operate or integrate through Amazon management console because the interface may change even if you create an instruction and capture several images for it. We learn how to create a static website with **Amazon Command Line Interface (AWS CLI)**. You need to meet the following requirements:

▶ Install and set up AWS CLI on your PC at `http://aws.amazon.com/cli/`

▶ Configure an IAM user and a policy to enable full access to S3 and issue an IAM credential

For more information about how to install and set up AWS CLI, refer to `https://github.com/aws/aws-cli`.

On the other hand, one of the easiest ways to use AWS CLI is to launch Amazon AMI because AWS CLI is installed in the AMI by default.

How to do it...

Proceed with the following steps to configure a static website on Amazon S3 bucket with AWS CLI. First, we create a bucket, configure the bucket as a website, put a bucket policy, and then upload objects using AWS CLI (`aws s3` and `aws s3api`).

1. Create and confirm a bucket.

```
$ aws s3 mbs3://<your_bucket> --region <region_name>
```

For example:

```
$ aws s3 mb s3://hashnao.info --region ap-northeast-1
```

If you do not specify a region, a bucket is created in the standard US region.

For a list of the regions supported by Amazon S3, refer to the URL `http://docs.aws.amazon.com/general/latest/gr/rande.html#s3_region`.

2. Configure a bucket as a website:

```
$ aws s3 website s3://<your_bucket> --index-document
<index_file> --error-document <error_file> --region
<region_name>
```

For example:

```
$ aws s3 website s3://s3test.hashnao.info/ --index-document
index.html --error 404.html --region ap-northeast-1
```

3. Create a bucket policy in JSON format and add the policy to a bucket:

```
$ cat > policy.json <<EOF
{
  "Version":"2012-10-17",
  "Statement":[{
    "Sid":"PublicReadGetObjects",
    "Effect":"Allow",
    "Principal": {
       "AWS": "*"
},
    "Action":["s3:GetObject"],
    "Resource":["arn:aws:s3:::<your_bucket>/*"
]
  }]
}
EOF
$ awss3api put-bucket-policy --bucket s3://<your_bucket> --policy
file://<your_policy>.json --region <region_name>
```

For example:

```
$ aws s3api put-bucket-policy --bucket hashnao.info --policy
file://policy.json --region ap-northeast-1
```

4. Get the website configuration for a bucket:

```
$ aws s3api get-bucket-website --bucket <your_bucket> --region
<region_name>
```

For example:

```
$ aws s3api get-bucket-website --bucket hashnao.info --region ap-
northeast-1
```

5. Upload your content into the bucket:

    ```
    $ aws s3 sync <your_document_directory>/ s3://<your_bucket> --
    region <region_name>
    ```

    For example:

    ```
    $ aws s3 syncmy_doc_dir/ s3://hashnao.info --region ap-
    northeast-1
    ```

How it works...

You can confirm whether a website on Amazon S3 bucket is available in the same way, as the instruction given in the *How to configure a static website on Amazon S3 bucket* recipe, in the browser.

See also

- ► AWS CLI document, available at `http://docs.aws.amazon.com/cli/latest/`

- ► AWS CLI (s3), available at `http://docs.aws.amazon.com/cli/latest/reference/s3/index.html`

- ► AWS CLI (s3api), available at `http://docs.aws.amazon.com/cli/latest/reference/s3api/index.html`

3

Calculating Cost with the AWS Simple Monthly Calculator

This chapter aims to teach you how to calculate the total cost of storing data and delivering objects through S3 with the Amazon Web Services Simple Monthly Calculator (the AWS calculator). For example, assuming how much it costs when simply delivering your media files such as images, streaming files through S3, or hosting a static website on a bucket in a month. You'll also learn how to record and manage AWS costs.

In this chapter, you will learn:

- ▶ To calculate and estimate S3 costs with the AWS calculator
- ▶ To annotate S3 billing by adding cost allocation tagging

Introduction

The AWS calculator is a web simulation tool to calculate AWS services. Anyone, even those who have not registered on AWS, can use the AWS calculator, estimate costs, and save the result that specifies its URL anytime. You do not have to use your own format or formula to estimate AWS costs.

In addition, several common customer samples are available on the right side on the calculator website, for example, a marketing website composed of S3 and CloudFront or a 3-Tier auto-scalable web application composed of EC2, S3, Route 53, CloudFront, RDS, DynamoDB, and so on. If you find it difficult to calculate on your own at first, you can view the customer scenarios and use them as templates.

The AWS calculator is available at `http://calculator.s3.amazonaws.com/index.html`.

How to calculate and estimate S3 costs with the AWS calculator

This section introduces the S3 pricing model and see how the cost differs following three scenarios; the first scenario is an assumption that download and upload requests accessing for contents on an S3 bucket, the second one is download and upload requests for Standard Storage and Reduced Redundancy Storage, and the third one is the same requests for an mixed environment with S3 and CloudFront.

Getting ready

Before using the AWS calculator, you need to learn about the Amazon S3 pricing model. Mainly, the S3 price comprises storage, requests, and data transfer and it differs by region (based on the location of your S3 bucket). Let's examine storage pricing, request pricing, and data transfer pricing shown at the official site, assuming that we use the US standard region and there is no AWS free tier in place.

The following table will show you the storage pricing of Amazon S3:

Data Transfer (month)	Standard Storage (per GB)	Reduced Standard Storage (per GB)
First 1 TB	$0.0300	$0.0240
Next 49 TB	$0.0295	$0.0236
Next 450 TB	$0.0290	$0.0232
Next 500 TB	$0.0285	$0.0228
Next 4000 TB	$0.0280	$0.0224
Over 5000 TB	$0.0275	$0.0220

Let's assume you store 52,900 GB a month; the storage pricing will be calculated as follows:

- For the first 1 TB (1,024 GB), storage pricing is $0.0300 per GB. So, the calculation for a 1 TB tier will be *1024 GB * $0.03000 = $30.72.*

- For the next 49 TB (*49 * 1024 = 50,176 GB*), storage pricing is $0.0295 per GB. So, the calculation from 1 TB to 50 TB tier will be *50,176 GB (49×1024) * $0.0295 = $1,480.19.*

- For the next 450 TB (*52,900 - 1024 + 50,176 = 1,700 GB*), storage pricing is $0.0290 per GB. So, the calculation from 50 TB to 450 TB tier will be *1,700 GB (remainder) * $0.0290 = $49.30.*

Thus, the total storage fee will be *$30.72 + $1,480.19 + $49.30 = $1,560.21.*

The following table will show you the request pricing of Amazon S3:

Request Type	Pricing
PUT, COPY, POST, or LIST Requests	$0.005 per 1,000 requests
Glacier Archive and Restore Requests	$0.05 per 1,000 requests
Delete Requests	Free
GET and all other Requests	$0.004 per 10,000 requests
Glacier Data Restores	Free

Assume that you transfer 10,000 files into Amazon S3 buckets and transfer 20,000 files out of the buckets each day during the month, and then delete 5,000 files at the end of the month, the request pricing will be calculated as follows:

- Total PUT requests will be *10,000 requests * 31 days = 310,000 requests*
- Total GET requests will be *20,000 requests * 31 days = 620,000 requests*
- Total DELETE requests will be *5,000 * 1 day = 5,000 requests*

The total request fee will be as follows:

- PUT requests will be *310,000 requests * $0.005/1,000 = $1.55*
- GET requests will be *620,000 requests * $0.004/10,000 = $0.25*
- DELETE requests will be *5,000 requests * $0.00 (no charge) = $0.00*

The following table will show you the data transfer pricing of Amazon S3:

Data Transfer	Pricing (per GB)
IN To Amazon S3	
All data transfer in	$0.000
OUT From Amazon S3 To	
Amazon EC2 in the Northern Virginia Region	$0.000
Another AWS Region	$0.020
Amazon CloudFront	$0.000
OUT From Amazon S3 To Internet	
First 1 GB / month	$0.000
Up to 10 TB / month	$0.090

Data Transfer	Pricing (per GB)
Next 40 TB / month	$0.085
Next 100 TB / month	$0.070
Next 350 TB / month	$0.050
Next 524 TB / month	Contact the Amazon Web Services sales representative
Next 4 PB / month	Contact the Amazon Web Services sales representative
Greater than 5 PB / month	Contact the Amazon Web Services sales representative

Assume that you transfer 1 TB of data out of your S3 buckets to the Internet every day for a 31-day month. The data transfer pricing will be calculated as follows:

▶ For 10 TB tier, it will be *10,240 GB (10 * 1024 GB) * $0.090 = $921.51*

▶ For 10 TB to 50 TB tier, it will be *21,504 GB (21 * 1024 GB) * $0.085 = $1,827.84*

The total data transfer fee will be *$921.51 + $1,827.84 = $2,749.35*.

 Data Transfer Out (From S3 to Internet) is charged, Data Transfer In (To S3) is free of charge.

The S3 price is calculated based on the US standard region, if the region is not specified, and the pricing list at January 24, 2015. See the details about S3 pricing at `http://aws.amazon.com/s3/pricing/`.

 An AWS price reduction occasionally occurs and it has reduced prices 42 times so far (March 26, 2014). Visit `https://aws.amazon.com/blogs/aws/aws-price-reduction-42-ec2-s3-rds-elasticache-and-elastic-mapreduce/`.

How to do it...

We will use the following examples to estimate the monthly S3 pricing, compare the costs, and see how it differs if we choose different regions for each condition.

Assume that we provide a web service in which users can send their pictures through an application into S3 buckets. We have 1,000,000 users, and the media file per request is about 1 MB on average, 900,000 uploads a day (30 percent of users upload 3 times a day), 5,000,000 requests (50 percent of users get 10 times a day).

Let's summarize the conditions, considering that we have 1,000,000 users and we need to do the following:

- **PUT requests (Uploads)**: 27,000,000 a month (*1,000,000 users * 30% * 3 times * 30 days = 27,000,000 requests*)

- **GET requests**: 150,000,000 a month (*1,000,000 users * 50% * 10 times * 30 days = 150,000,000 requests*)

- **Data transfer**: 1 MB per request

The first example

We have an S3 bucket containing contents such as media files or images and our users upload their contents into the bucket and retrieve the contents through the bucket.

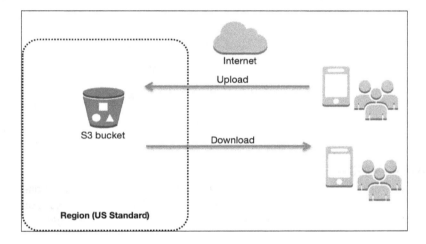

The second example

We have an S3 bucket composed of Standard Storage and Reduced Redundancy Storage (RRS) containing media files and our users upload their contents into the bucket and retrieve the contents through the bucket.

Storage and Reduced Redundancy Storage (**RRS**) has less durability and availability than standard storage (RRS is designed for 99.99 percent durability of objects over a given year), but costs lower than standard storage by 80 percent. For more information about RRS, visit `https://docs.aws. amazon.com/AmazonS3/latest/dev/UsingRRS.html`.

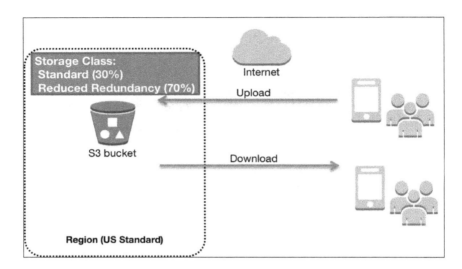

The third example

In the same environment as the second example, we have an S3 bucket composed of Storage and Reduced Redundancy Storage (RRS) containing media files, and our users upload their contents into the bucket and retrieve the contents in the bucket through CloudFront distribution all over.

 CloudFront is a Content Delivery Service that speeds up your content by caching and distributing your content through edge locations around the world. For more information about CloudFront, visit `http://aws.amazon. com/cloudfront/`.

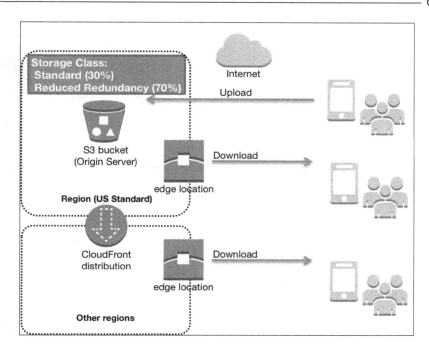

First, let's examine the following table that reflects the conditions of each example; we will explore the details later. We use the following parameter to estimate S3 costs (the third condition involves CloudFront):

		First	Second	Third	
Amazon S3					
	Storage				
	Storage	27,000	8,100	8,100	GB
	Reduced Redundancy Storage	0	18,900	18,900	GB
	Requests				
	PUT/COPY/POST/LIST Requests	27,000,000	27,000,000	27,000,000	Requests
	GET and Other Requests	150,000,000	150,000,000	0	Requests
	Data Transfer				
	Inter-Region Data Transfer Out:	0	0	27,000	GB
	Data Transfer Out:	150,000	150,000	0	GB
	Data Transfer In:	27,000	27,000	27,000	GB

			First	Second	Third	
CloudFront						
	Data Transfer Out					
		Monthly Volume	0	0	150,000	GB
	Requests					
		Average Object Size	0	0	1,000	KB
		Type of Requests			HTTP	HTTP or HTTPS
		Invalidation Requests	0	0	0	Requests
	Edge Location Traffic Distribution					
		United States	0	0	40	%
		Europe	0	0	10	%
		Hong Kong, Philippines, S. Korea, Singapore, and Taiwan	0	0	15	%
		Japan	0	0	20	%
		South America	0	0	0	%
		Australia	0	0	5	%
		India	0	0	10	%
	Dedicated IP SSL Certificates					
		Number of Certificates	0	0	0	

The following part focuses on how to use the AWS calculator. Let's try to calculate using the first example:

1. Type the URL (`http://calculator.s3.amazonaws.com/index.html`) in your browser and open the AWS calculator.

2. In the **Language** box on the right, choose the language in which you want to display it.

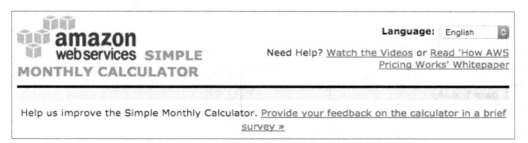

3. In the **Service** section, choose **Amazon S3**.

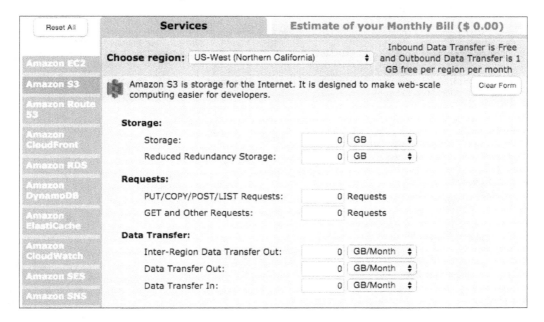

4. In the **Choose region** box, choose the region in which you want to calculate the cost.

5. Then, as shown in the following screenshot, add numbers in the **Storage**, **Requests**, and **Data Transfer** sections:

Choose region: US-East / US Standard (Virginia) ⬍   Inbound Data Transfer is Free and Outbound Data Transfer is 1 GB free per region per month

Amazon S3 is storage for the Internet. It is designed to make web-scale computing easier for developers.   Clear Form

Storage:

Storage:	27000	GB ⬍
Reduced Redundancy Storage:	0	GB ⬍

Requests:

PUT/COPY/POST/LIST Requests:	2700000C	Requests
GET and Other Requests:	1500000C	Requests

Data Transfer:

Inter-Region Data Transfer Out:	0	GB/Month ⬍
Data Transfer Out:	150000	GB/Month ⬍
Data Transfer In:	27000	GB/Month ⬍

6. Choose the **Estimate of your Monthly Bill ($ 12311.13)** tab as shown in the following screenshot. You will see that your monthly bill appears.

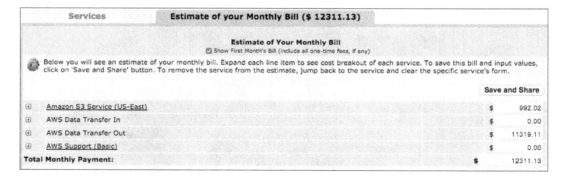

Services	Estimate of your Monthly Bill ($ 12311.13)	

Estimate of Your Monthly Bill
☑ Show First Month's Bill (include all one-time fees, if any)

Below you will see an estimate of your monthly bill. Expand each line item to see cost breakout of each service. To save this bill and input values, click on 'Save and Share' button. To remove the service from the estimate, jump back to the service and clear the specific service's form.

		Save and Share
⊞	Amazon S3 Service (US-East)	$ 992.02
⊞	AWS Data Transfer In	$ 0.00
⊞	AWS Data Transfer Out	$ 11319.11
⊞	AWS Support (Basic)	$ 0.00
Total Monthly Payment:		$ 12311.13

7. To see the cost breakout of each service, expand each line item. You can do that by clicking on the highlighted icon in the following screenshot:

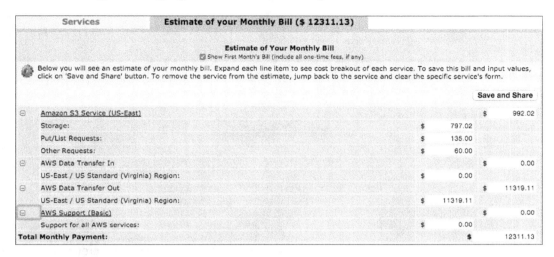

8. To save your billing, click on **Save and Share**, then click on **OK**. As you can see in the following screenshot, it is mentioned that **All fields are Optional**.

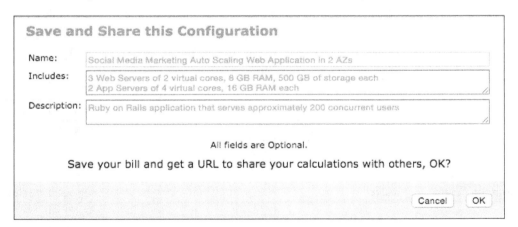

9. After clicking on **OK**, the URL for your calculations is generated.

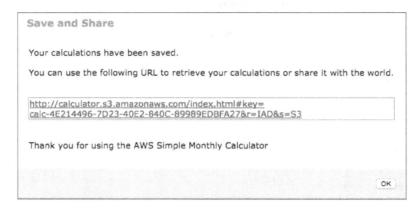

How it works...

As you learned about how to simulate S3 pricing with the AWS calculator in the previous section, we will now examine the examples to see how much they cost in total and how much each component (such as storage pricing, request pricing, and data transfer pricing) costs.

The following table shows the overall IT costs for each example, using the AWS calculator:

	First		Second		Third	
Amazon S3 Service (US-East)		992		881		1,360
Storage:	797		239		239	
Reduced Redundancy Storage:	0		446		446	
Put/List Requests:	135		135		135	
GET and Other Requests:	60		60		0	
Inter-Region Data Transfer Out	0		0		540	
Amazon CloudFront Service		0		0		16,658
Data Transfer Out:	0		0		16,525	
Requests:	0		0		132	
AWS Data Transfer In		0		0		0
US-East / US Standard (Virginia) Region:	0		0		0	
AWS Data Transfer Out		11,319		11,319		0
US-East / US Standard (Virginia) Region:	11,319		11,319		0	
Total Monthly Payment:	$12,311		$12,200		$18,018	

Let's get to the nitty-gritty about the S3 pricing model:

▸ **Data Transfer Pricing**: Data transfer Out is the most expensive, and 90 percent of the overall cost is Data Transfer Out. (The total payment of the first example is $12,311 and its Data Transfer Out is $11,319; the second example's total payment is $12,200 and its Data Transfer Out is the same). Data transfer In is free (described as $0.000 per GB in the official S3 price list).

▸ **Data Transfer Pricing (CloudFront)**: Data Transfer Out through CloudFront is about 160 percent compared to that of S3. This is because the CloudFront pricing differs by regions, as with S3 Data Transfer Out. We will see details about the CloudFront pricing in the next chapter. (Data Transfer Out in the third example is $16,525, as opposed to are $11,319 in the second and third examples.)

▸ **Storage Pricing**: The price of RRS designed for 99.99 percent durability is about 80 percent of Standard Storage designed for 99.999999999 percent durability. (The S3 Storage payment for the first example is $797, that of the second example is $239, and the RRS payment for the second one is $446.)

▸ **Request Pricing**: The request payment is simple because it is based on the formula. The Put/List requests payment for all the examples is $135 (*27,000,000 requests / 1,000 * 0.005 = $135*). The GET and Other Requests payment for all the examples is $60 (*150,000,000 requests / 10,000 * 0.004 = $60*).

PUT, COPY, POST, or LIST Requests	$0.005 per 1,000 requests
GET and all other Requests	$0.004 per 10,000 requests

You can see the actual estimation for all examples with the AWS calculator on the following links:

▸ `http://calculator.s3.amazonaws.com/index.html#key=calc-FD1456C2-D8E7-4BB9-88FF-59E50CF0B85C`

▸ `http://calculator.s3.amazonaws.com/index.html#key=calc-C5282EB2-3DF7-42AC-93CF-3E36CB7D2BDE`

▸ `http://calculator.s3.amazonaws.com/index.html#key=calc-2282111D-916F-4AB7-B859-993FE1EF251F`

There's more...

Let's compare the overall IT costs with other regions to see how much they differ by region between the first, second, and third example. The following table shows the overall IT costs for each example by region:

	First		Second		Third	
Amazon S3 Service (US-East)		992		881		1,361
Amazon S3 Service (US-West-2)		992		881		1,361
Amazon S3 Service (US-West)		1,090		968		1,442
Amazon S3 Service (Europe)		992		881		1,361
Amazon S3 Service (Europe Central)		1,072		952		1,427
Amazon S3 Service (Singapore)		992		912		3,251
Amazon S3 Service (Japan)		1,058		935		3,310
Amazon S3 Service (Sydney)		1,090		968		4,682
Amazon S3 Service (South America)		1,356		1,204		5,440
Amazon S3 Service (GovCloud-US)		1,230		1,085		1,835
Amazon CloudFront Service		0		0		18,934
AWS Data Transfer In		0		0		0
AWS Data Transfer Out		156,940		156,940		0
US-East / US Standard (Virginia) Region	11,319		11,319		0	
US-West-2 (Oregon) Region	11,319		11,319		0	
US-West (Northern California) Region	11,319		11,319		0	
Europe (Ireland) Region	11,319		11,319		0	
Europe Central (Frankfurt) Region	11,319		11,319		0	
Asia Pacific (Singapore) Region	12,812		12,812		0	
Asia Pacific (Japan) Region	19,807		19,807		0	
Asia Pacific (Sydney) Region	19,807		19,807		0	
South America (Sao Paulo) Region	32,729		32,728		0	
AWS GovCloud (US) Region	15,189		15,189		0	
Total Monthly Payment	**$167,804**		**$166,606**		**$44,403**	

To summarize, the reasons why the costs differ by region are mainly the following:

- **Data Transfer Pricing**: Data Transfer Out pricing clearly differs by region. (The South America region is the most expensive and its payment is $32,729. US-East, US-West, US-West-2, Europe, and Europe Central are the lowest and their payments are $11,319.)

- **Amazon S3 Service**: The reason why Storage pricing differs by region is the same as Data Transfer Pricing. (The exact number is not shown in the preceding table, but the South America region is the most expensive and its payment is $1,083. US-East, US-West-2, Europe, and Singapore are the lowest and their payments are $797.)

  When using CloudFront, Inter-Region Data Transfer Out is needed to transfer from the origin data (S3 bucket) to CloudFront distribution and the price differs greatly from US, EU, and Asia regions. (Inter-Region Data Transfer Out is not described here; check the AWS calculator URL later.)

You can see the actual estimation for all examples with the AWS calculator on the following links:

- `http://calculator.s3.amazonaws.com/index.html#key=calc-FE8EA478-0C72-4D6A-983B-5237969BD626`

- `http://calculator.s3.amazonaws.com/index.html#key=calc-58555E43-C719-4335-86A6-4250138C76E3`

- `http://calculator.s3.amazonaws.com/index.html#key=calc-0ECE2CF5-21D4-4BE0-A160-BCE68D08C0D3`

See also

- Amazon S3 Pricing `http://aws.amazon.com/s3/pricing/`
- The AWS calculator Common Customer Samples `http://calculator.s3.amazonaws.com/index.html`. You can refer to several samples in the **Common Customer Samples** section (the section on the right)

How to annotate S3 billing by adding cost allocation tagging

Cost allocation tagging is to label your S3 buckets with a tag that consists of a key and a value in order to track their costs. Of course, cost allocation tagging is used also for other AWS resources such as EC2 instances, EBS volumes, RDS, and so on.

Getting ready

You need to enable Detailed Billing reports and set up your monthly cost allocation report by following the official instructions in advance:

▶ *Understand Your Usage with Detailed Billing Reports*: `http://docs.aws.amazon.com/awsaccountbilling/latest/aboutv2/detailed-billing-reports.html`

▶ *Setting Up Your Monthly Cost Allocation Reports*: `http://docs.aws.amazon.com/awsaccountbilling/latest/aboutv2/configurecostallocreport.html`

How to do it...

After enabling Detailed Billing reports and setting up your monthly cost allocation report, you need to add a tag on your S3 bucket with a key and a value in the S3 console, and then choose and enable your cost allocation tags in the billing console:

1. Sign in to the AWS management console and open the S3 console at `https://console.aws.amazon.com/s3`.

2. In the bucket list, click on the bucket name, and then click on **Tags** from the properties:

3. Click on **Add more tags**.

4. In **Key** box and the **Value** boxes, input your key and value, and then click on **Save**.

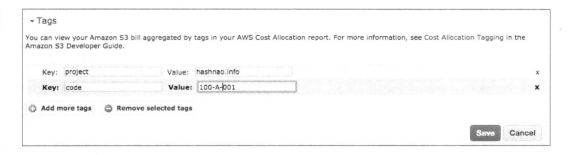

5. Open the billing console at https://console.aws.amazon.com/billing/home#/.

6. Then, from the navigation panel on the left, select **Preferences**.

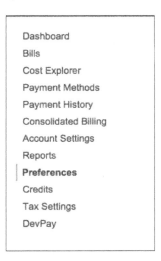

7.   In the detailed report section, click on **Manage report tags**.

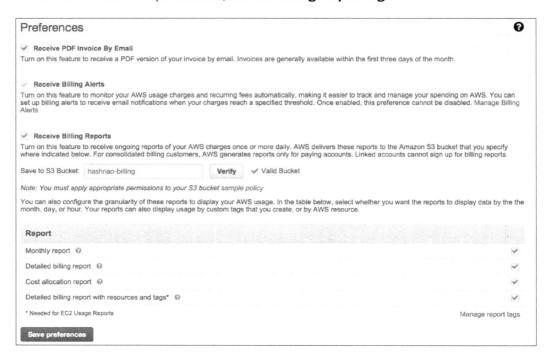

8.   Select the tags that you want to enable, and click on **Save**.

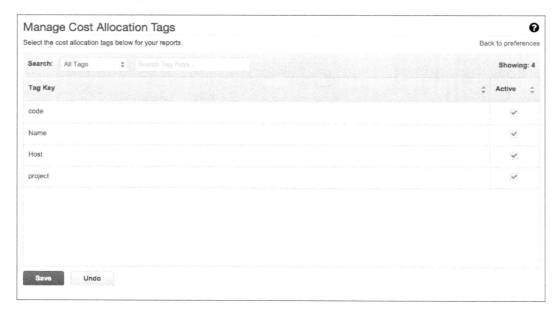

How it works...

You can view your billing cost allocation report in your S3 bucket.

Total Cost	user:Owner	user:Stack	user:Cost Center	user:Application
0.95	DbAdmin	Test	80432	Widget2
0.01	DbAdmin	Test	80432	Widget2
3.84	DbAdmin	Prod	80432	Widget2
6.00	DbAdmin	Test	78925	Widget1
234.63	SysEng	Prod	78925	Widget1
0.73	DbAdmin	Test	78925	Widget1
0.00	DbAdmin	Prod	80432	Portal
2.47	DbAdmin	Prod	78925	Portal

 It can take up 24 hours for AWS to start delivering detailed billing report files to your S3 bucket. See http://docs.aws.amazon.com/ awsaccountbilling/latest/aboutv2/detailed-billing- reports.html.

See also

▶ *Billing and Reporting of Buckets*: http://docs.aws.amazon.com/AmazonS3/ latest/dev/BucketBilling.html

▶ *Viewing a Cost Allocation Report*: http://docs.aws.amazon.com/ awsaccountbilling/latest/aboutv2/configurecostallocreport. html#allocation-viewing

4

Deploying a Static Website with CloudFormation

In this chapter, you will learn:

- ▶ How to deploy a template of a static website with CloudFormation
- ▶ How to deploy a template with the AWS CLI

Introduction

CloudFormation is a deployment tool that helps to provision your infrastructure using AWS resources such as EC2, IAM, RDS, Route 53, S3, and so on by creating a template to code your infrastructure in it so that you can deploy your infrastructure repeatedly. An AWS CloudFormation template is a text file and its format is the JSON standard and all the resources in the template are a single unit called stack. For example, imagine that you need to design and integrate a typical 3-tier web system with VPC, EC2, EBS, RDS, Route53, and ELB to deploy a system through the AWS management console or using AWS CLI. It will take several steps and probably a couple of hours at least, to finish your operation. If you code your infrastructure and create a CloudFormation template, you can deploy the infrastructure repeatedly and delete it as well.

In *Chapter 2, Hosting a Static Website on Amazon S3 Bucket,* we manually configured a static website on the S3 bucket through the S3 management console. Now, we will try to deploy the same environment creating a CloudFormation template, as shown in the following diagram:

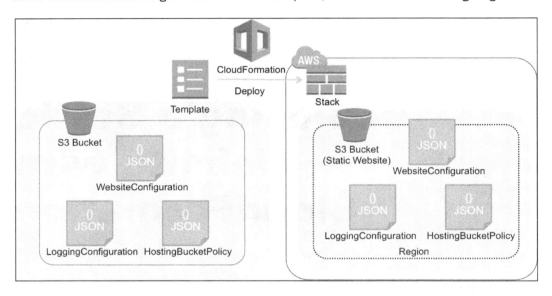

How to deploy a template of a static website with CloudFormation

In *Chapter 2, Hosting a Static Website on Amazon S3 Bucket,* you learned how to host a static website on S3 bucket through the AWS management console and AWS CLI. To simplify and code the infrastructure, we use CloudFormation to deploy the same environment of the S3 bucket with a static website.

After deploying the template, we will look into the template to understand how it works and how to write a CloudFormation template.

Getting ready

You do not need to request or fill any form to use CloudFormation, or pay any initial or extra cost. All you need to do is sign up on the AWS management console and access CloudFormation using your IAM credentials.

There is no additional charge for CloudFormation itself, but you need to pay for AWS resources when you manually create your AWS resource. Visit http://aws.amazon.com/cloudformation/pricing/.

How to do it...

First of all, we will select a template specifying a template URL on Amazon S3, and define a few parameters, and then begin to create a stack with the template. We can upload a template, but it is much easier just to specify a URL because you do not need to download and upload a template:

1. Sign in to the AWS management console and move it to the CloudFormation console at https://console.aws.amazon.com/cloudformation.

2. You can see the **Create New Stack** button at the bottom of the screen, just click on it.

3. Then in the **Name** box, input a stack name. In the template box, choose **Specify an Amazon S3 template URL**, and input the URL (https://s3-ap-northeast-1. amazonaws.com/hashnao.info/CloudFormation/S3Hosting.json), and then Click on **Next**.

It is also possible to download the template and upload it to Amazon S3 by choosing **Upload a template to Amazon S3**, but it creates a temporary bucket to store the template and it remains. On the other hand, it will not create a temporary bucket by specifying an Amazon S3 template URL.

4. In the **HostingBucketName** box, input a bucket name for a static website bucket. In the **LoggingBucketName** box, input a bucket name for a server access logging bucket, and then click on **Next**.

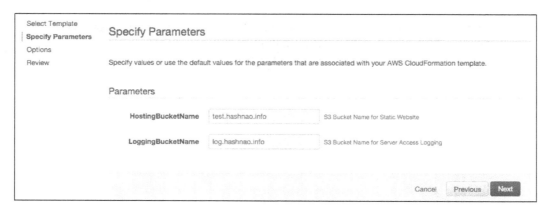

In *Chapter 2, Hosting a Static Website on Amazon S3 Bucket*, we used the same bucket for a static website by specifying a target prefix under the bucket to store server access logging. However, we will be creating another bucket for server access logging to separate your contents and access log files in the different bucket, here.

5. Skip the **Options** section, and Click on **Next**.

 In the **Tags** section, you can put **Key** and **Value** as a tag for the resource in order to name the stack, for example, `my-s3-website` or `s3-static-website`, but you also can skip this and just click on the **Next** button, as tags are optional.

> In the advanced section, you can use notification options to notify stack events using Amazon **Simple Notification Service** (**SNS**). This is optional. For more details see `https://docs.aws.amazon.com/AWSCloudFormation/latest/UserGuide/cfn-console-add-tags.html`.

6. Review the parameters in the **Parameters** section, and then click on **Create**.

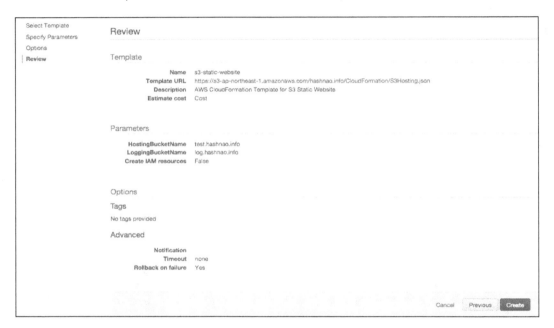

> You can go back to the previous sections if you want to correct the parameters clicking on the **Previous** button.

How it works...

Let's confirm whether the stack is successfully created step by step. After clicking on the **Create** button, CloudFormation initiates a type called `AWS::CloudFormation::Stack` and begins to create each resource in the template. During the sequence, CloudFormation shows each status for the resources and if it fails to create one of the resources, CloudFormation will automatically begin to roll back and delete all the related resources.

If it succeeds to create all the resources, the status of `AWS::CloudFormation::Stack` moves to `CREATE_COMPLETE`:

1. After a couple of minutes, `CREATE_COMPLTE` appears in the **Status** section if it succeeds as follows.

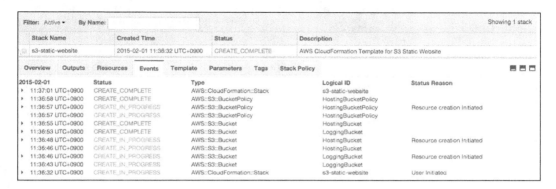

2. Click on the **Outputs** tab, then you can see the website endpoint, the bucket names for a static website, and server access logging.

3. You can move to the S3 console at `https://console.aws.amazon.com/s3` or use AWS CLI to list the buckets.

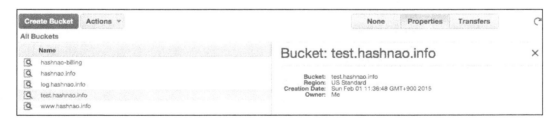

4. If you use the AWS CLI and `aws s3` subcommand, you can list the bucket as follows:

```
$ aws s3 ls 2015-02-01 11:36:47 log.hashnao.info
2015-02-01 11:36:58 test.hashnao.info
```

Finally, let's look into the template in which we created the bucket and see how it works at `https://s3-ap-northeast-1.amazonaws.com/hashnao.info/CloudFormation/S3Hosting.json`.

In the `Parameters` section, it declares two bucket names for a static website and server access logging, and the `Default` property defines a value for their bucket name as a constraint for the parameter called `your_website_bucket`:

```
"Parameters": {
  "HostingBucketName": {
    "Type" : "String",
    "Description": "S3 Bucket Name for Static Website",
    "Default" : "your_website_bucket"
  },
  "LoggingBucketName": {
    "Type" : "String",
    "Description": "S3 Bucket Name for Server Access Logging",
    "Default" : "your_logging_bucket"
  }
},
```

In the Resources section, it declares two buckets with the `AWS::S3::Bucket` property and a bucket policy with the `AWS::S3::BucketPolicy` property as follows:

- `HostingBucket` defines a bucket for a static website, the access control as public read, website configuration for index document and error document, and the destination bucket for server access logging and its prefix

- `LoggingBucket` defines a bucket for server access logging and access control as a log-delivery write that needs to be added to enable server access logging

- `HostingBucketPolicy` defines a bucket policy for the static website bucket to allow public read access for the `S3::GetObject` method:

```
"Resources" : {
  "HostingBucket" : {
    "Type" : "AWS::S3::Bucket",
    "Properties" : {
      "BucketName" : { "Ref" : "HostingBucketName" },
      "AccessControl": "PublicRead",
      "WebsiteConfiguration" : {
        "IndexDocument" : "index.html",
        "ErrorDocument" : "error.html"
```

```
          },
          "LoggingConfiguration": {
            "DestinationBucketName": { "Ref" : "LoggingBucketName"
            },
            "LogFilePrefix": "logs/"
          }
        }
      },
      "LoggingBucket": {
        "Type": "AWS::S3::Bucket",
        "Properties": {
          "BucketName" : { "Ref" : "LoggingBucketName" },
          "AccessControl": "LogDeliveryWrite"
        }
      },
      "HostingBucketPolicy" : {
        "Type" : "AWS::S3::BucketPolicy",
        "Properties" : {
          "PolicyDocument" : {
            "Version" : "2012-10-17",
            "Id" : "PublicReadGet",
            "Statement" : [ {
              "Sid" : "ReadAccess",
              "Action" : [ "s3:GetObject" ],
              "Effect" : "Allow",
              "Resource" : { "Fn::Join" : ["", ["arn:aws:s3:::", {
              "Ref" : "HostingBucket" } , "/*" ] ] },
              "Principal" : "*"
            } ]
          },
          "Bucket" : { "Ref" : "HostingBucket" }
        }
      }
```

In the `Outputs` section, it declares three properties for the website endpoint called `S3HostingBucketEndpoint`, the static website bucket name called `S3HostingBucketName`, and the server access logging bucket name called `ServerAccessLoggingBucketName`.

`S3HostingBucketEndpoint` will be `https://HostingBucket.s3.amazonaws.com/` concatenated by the `Fn::Join` function.

The `Fn::Join` function defined as the value for `S3HostingBucketEndpoint` concatenates a set of values separated by the specified delimiter. For more information about `Fn::Join`, see https://docs.aws.amazon.com/AWSCloudFormation/latest/UserGuide/intrinsic-function-reference-join.html.

```
"Outputs" : {
  "S3HostingBucketEndpoint" : {
    "Value" : { "Fn::Join" : ["", [ "https://", { "Ref" :
    "HostingBucket" }, ".s3.amazonaws.com/" ] ] }
  },
  "S3HostingBucketName" : {
    "Value" : { "Ref" : "HostingBucket" }
  },
  "ServerAccessLoggingBucketName" : {
    "Value" : { "Ref" : "LoggingBucket" }
  }
}
```

The properties in the output show up at the **Outputs** tab after creating a stack in the CloudFormation console as follows:

Filter: Active ▾	By Name:			Showing 1 stack
Stack Name	Created Time	Status	Description	
s3-static-website	2015-02-01 11:36:32 UTC+0900	CREATE_COMPLETE	AWS CloudFormation Template for S3 Static Website	

Overview	Outputs	Resources	Events	Template	Parameters	Tags	Stack Policy		

Key	Value	Description
S3HostingBucketEndpoint	https://test.hashnao.info.s3.amazonaws.com/	
S3HostingBucketName	test.hashnao.info	
ServerAccessLoggingBucketName	log.hashnao.info	

There's more...

Unfortunately, there are several situations that you launch a stack, but the stack does not complete creating each resource and rolls back, for example, if the IAM permission for creating resources is insufficient or there are invalid or unsupported parameters in the template. We will see and examine a scenario in which a stack fails to launch because of insufficient IAM permissions.

Why CloudFormation failed to create a stack

This is one of the examples when CloudFormation failed to create a stack. Let's see why it failed by uploading the following template and following each resource status and status reason in the **Events** tab:

```
https://s3-ap-northeast-1.amazonaws.com/hashnao.info/CloudFormation/
S3Hosting_resource_err.json
```

After beginning to create a stack, the status of a stack called `s3-static-website` finally became **ROLLBACK_COMPLETE**.

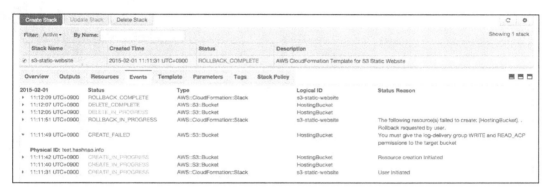

The following status defines the details shown in the preceding screenshot:

- ► **ROLLBACK_COMPLETE**: This indicates that all the related resources in the template were successfully deleted and went back to the stage before creating the stack

- ► **DELETE_COMPLETE**: This finished deleting all the related resources

- ► **DELETE_IN_PROGRESS**: This begins to delete all the related resources

- ► **ROLLBACK_IN_PROGRESS**: This enters a roll back sequence because of the previous event

- ► **CREATE_FAILED**: This is the very reason why the stack failed

In the **Status Reason** column, you will see **You must give the log-delivery group WRITE and READ_ACP permissions to the target bucket**. The reason why it failed is that I forgot to create and add a permission of server access logging to the bucket in the template, and the stack failed to create and rollback begins. In the CloudFormation, a function called automatic rollback on error is enabled by default.

If you need to examine how the stack failed without rolling up, you can disable rollback on failure while creating a stack, as shown in the following screen. In the **Options** section, click on **Advanced** and then click on **No** in the **Rollback on failure** section.

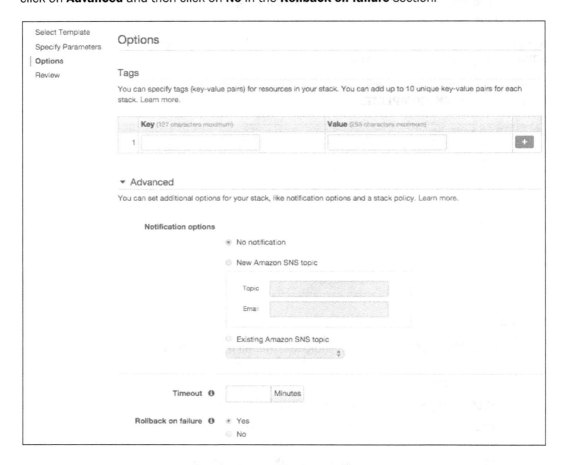

Deleting a stack

After successfully creating a stack, you might also need to delete all the resources in the template because the project is finished or the website is closing. To delete a stack is very simple, just specify the stack and click on one button. That's all.

1. Sign in to the AWS management console and move to the CloudFormation console at `https://console.aws.amazon.com/cloudformation`.

2. Select the stack you want to delete and click on **Delete Stack**.

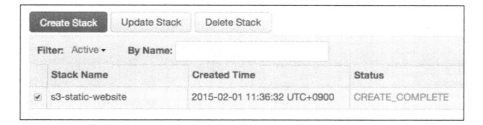

 Make sure that all of the objects are deleted before deleting the S3 bucket because S3 buckets, if any, cannot be deleted and CloudFormation cannot delete objects in a bucket.

3. The following popup will appear, and then, click on **Yes, Delete**.

4. The status becomes **DELETE_IN_PROGRESS**, as follows.

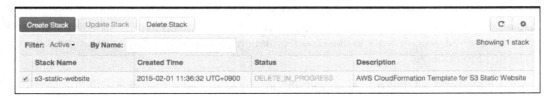

5. After succeeding to delete the stack, you can see the deleted stacks selecting **Deleted** in the **Filter** tab.

See also

▶ AWS CloudFormation Concepts available at `http://docs.aws.amazon.com/AWSCloudFormation/latest/UserGuide/cfn-whatis-concepts.html`

▶ Learn Template Basics available at `http://docs.aws.amazon.com/AWSCloudFormation/latest/UserGuide/gettingstarted.templatebasics.html`

▶ S3 Sample Template available at `http://docs.aws.amazon.com/AWSCloudFormation/latest/UserGuide/cfn-sample-templates.html`

How to deploy a template with AWS CLI

In *Chapter 2, Hosting a Static Website on Amazon S3 Bucket*, we used AWS CLI to create an S3 bucket as a static website. AWS CLI supports CloudFormation as well so that we can create a stack with only a command line.

Getting ready

As we have already used AWS CLI in *Chapter 2, Hosting a Static Website on Amazon S3 Bucket*, the requirement is the same as before. We just need to add a full CloudFront access policy for the IAM user. In order to use CloudFormation with AWS CLI, you need to meet the following requirements:

▶ Install and set up AWS CLI on your PC (`http://aws.amazon.com/cli/`)

▶ Configure an IAM user and a policy to enable full access to S3, full access to CloudFront, and issue an IAM credential.

For more information about how to install and set up AWS CLI, see
`https://github.com/aws/aws-cli`.

On the other hand, one of the easiest ways to use AWS CLI is to launch
Amazon AMI because AWS CLI is installed in the AMI by default.

How to do it...

After logging in to the environment where we can use AWS CLI, we will just type the following
commands instead of signing up to the CloudFormation console:

1. Set variables for a stack and template parameters:

   ```
   $ stack_name="<your_stack_name>"
   $ template_url="https://s3-ap-northeast-1.amazonaws.com/hashnao.
   info/CloudFormation/S3Hosting.json"
   $ HostingBucketName="<your_hosting_bucket>"
   $ LoggingBucketName="<your_logging_bucket>"
   ```

2. Validate a template using AWS CLI CloudFormation subcommand:

   ```
   $ aws cloudformation validate-template \
   --template-url ${template_url}
   ```

    CloudFormation does not support the dry-run mode, but
   automatically validates the template when uploaded or its
   URL is specified. Make sure that you check your template
   on your own before creating a stack.

   When it succeeds to validate a template, it responds to the parameters of the
   template as follows:

   ```
   {
       "Description": "AWS CloudFormation Template for S3 Static
   Website",
       "Parameters": [
           {
               "DefaultValue": "your_logging_bucket",
               "NoEcho": false,
               "Description": "S3 Bucket Name for Server Access
   Logging",
               "ParameterKey": "LoggingBucketName"
           },
           {
               "DefaultValue": "your_website_bucket",
   ```

```
                              "NoEcho": false,
                              "Description": "S3 Bucket Name for Static Website",
                              "ParameterKey": "HostingBucketName"
                      }
                  ]
          }
```

3. Create a stack using the following code:

```
$ aws cloudformation create-stack \
--stack-name ${stack_name} \
--template-url ${template_url} \
--parameters ParameterKey=HostingBucketName,ParameterValue=${Hosti
ngBucketName} \
ParameterKey=LoggingBucketName,ParameterValue=${LoggingBucketName}
```

When it succeeds to create a stack, it responds the stack ID as follows.

```
{
"StackId": "arn:aws:cloudformation:ap-northeast-
1:099897076573:stack/s3-statci-website/98b03ce0-a9e1-11e4-b04c-
50a676d45896"
}
```

How it works...

AWS CLI CloudFormation supports several subcommands such as describing a stack, describing stack events, getting a template for the stack, simply listing stacks. Let's see that the stack is created by checking the resource status with the subcommand, as we checked in the CloudFormation console as well in the previous section.

First, we will be listing the stacks whose status is CREATE_COMPLTE with the list-stacks subcommand. We can see that StackStatus is CREATE_COMPLTE:

```
$ aws cloudformation list-stacks \
--stack-status-filter CREATE_COMPLETE
{
    "StackSummaries": [
        {
"StackId": "arn:aws:cloudformation:ap-northeast-
1:099897076573:stack/s3-statci-website/98b03ce0-a9e1-11e4-b04c-
50a676d45896",
"TemplateDescription": "AWS CloudFormation Template for S3 Static
Website",
            "StackStatusReason": null,
            "CreationTime": "2015-02-01T07:11:52.420Z",
```

```
          "StackName": "s3-statci-website",
          "StackStatus": "CREATE_COMPLETE"
},
     ]
}
```

Let's see the details about the stack with the `describe-stack-resources` subcommand and check that all the resources are successfully created. We can see that `ResourceStatus` is `CREATE_COMPLTE`:

```
$ aws cloudformation describe-stack-resources --stack-name
${stack_name}
{
    "StackResources": [
{
          "StackId": "arn:aws:cloudformation:ap-northeast-
          1:099897076573:stack/s3-statci-website/98b03ce0-a9e1-
          11e4-b04c-50a676d45896",
          "ResourceStatus": "CREATE_COMPLETE",
          "ResourceType": "AWS::S3::Bucket",
          "Timestamp": "2015-02-01T07:12:08.107Z",
          "StackName": "s3-statci-website",
          "PhysicalResourceId": "log.hashnao.info",
          "LogicalResourceId": "LoggingBucket"
},
{
          "StackId": "arn:aws:cloudformation:ap-northeast-
          1:099897076573:stack/s3-statci-website/98b03ce0-a9e1-
          11e4-b04c-50a676d45896",
          "ResourceStatus": "CREATE_COMPLETE",
          "ResourceType": "AWS::S3::Bucket",
          "Timestamp": "2015-02-01T07:12:08.301Z",
          "StackName": "s3-statci-website",
          "PhysicalResourceId": "test.hashnao.info",
          "LogicalResourceId": "HostingBucket"
},
{
          "StackId": "arn:aws:cloudformation:ap-northeast-
          1:099897076573:stack/s3-statci-website/98b03ce0-a9e1-
          11e4-b04c-50a676d45896",
          "ResourceStatus": "CREATE_COMPLETE",
          "ResourceType": "AWS::S3::BucketPolicy",
          "Timestamp": "2015-02-01T07:12:11.761Z",
          "StackName": "s3-statci-website",
```

```
                "PhysicalResourceId": "s3-statci-website-
                HostingBucketPolicy-1UH18JTLNYFPX",
                "LogicalResourceId": "HostingBucketPolicy"
}
    ]
}
```

Deleting a stack

Let's delete an unnecessary resource to finish our verification, in the same way as we deleted a stack in the CloudFormation console before. When deleting a stack, the CLI shows no output unfortunately; we need to confirm that the stack is deleted by listing the deleted stack with other subcommand:

1. Delete a stack by using a subcommand called `delete-stack`:

    ```
    $ aws cloudformation delete-stack \
    --stack-name ${stack_name}
    ```

2. List the deleted stacks and confirm that the stack is deleted, using a subcommand called `list-stacks`:

    ```
    $ aws cloudformation list-stacks \
    --stack-status-filter DELETE_COMPLETE
    {
        "StackSummaries": [
            {
    "StackId": "arn:aws:cloudformation:ap-northeast-
    1:099897076573:stack/s3-static-website/fb2f5210-a9d8-11e4-
    8a0d-5088487c4896",
                "DeletionTime": "2015-02-01T06:55:15.244Z",
    "TemplateDescription": "AWS CloudFormation Template for S3
    Static Website",
                "StackStatusReason": "User Initiated",
                "CreationTime": "2015-02-01T06:10:12.189Z",
                "StackName": "s3-static-website",
                "StackStatus": "DELETE_COMPLETE"
    }
        ]
    }
    ```

Validating your template

In the CloudFormation console, CloudFormation outputs messages if your template has some syntax error or is missing some resources. You can check your template file for syntax error, as AWS CLI supports validating a template as well.

The following example shows no error message and all parameters listed. The result outputs all parameters without any syntax error:

```
$ aws cloudformation validate-template \
--template-url https://s3-ap-northeast-
1.amazonaws.com/hashnao.info/CloudFormation/S3Hosting.json
{
"Description": "AWS CloudFormation Template for S3 Static Website",
    "Parameters": [
{
    "DefaultValue": "your_logging_bucket",
    "NoEcho": false,
    "Description": "S3 Bucket Name for Server Access Logging",
    "ParameterKey": "LoggingBucketName"
},
{
    "DefaultValue": "your_website_bucket",
    "NoEcho": false,
    "Description": "S3 Bucket Name for Static Website",
    "ParameterKey": "HostingBucketName"
}
    ]
}
```

The following example shows that the template misses a resource called `BucketPolicy` `misses` and the message says so:

```
$ aws cloudformation validate-template \
--template-url https://s3-ap-northeast-
1.amazonaws.com/hashnao.info/CloudFormation/S3Hosting_resource_err.js
on

A client error (ValidationError) occurred when calling the
ValidateTemplate operation: Template format error: Unresolved
resource dependencies [LoggingBucketName] in the Resources block of
the template
```

The following example shows the template has a syntax error in the JSON format:

```
$ aws cloudformation validate-template \
--template-url https://s3-ap-northeast-1.amazonaws.com/hashnao.info/
CloudFormation/S3Hosting_syntax_err.json

A client error (ValidationError) occurred when calling the
ValidateTemplate operation: Template format error: JSON not well-
formed. (line 15, column 4)
```

See also

▸ AWS CLI cloudformation available at `http://docs.aws.amazon.com/cli/latest/reference/cloudformation/index.html`

▸ Validate Template available at `http://docs.aws.amazon.com/AWSCloudFormation/latest/APIReference/API_ValidateTemplate.html`

5

Distributing Your Contents via CloudFront

In this chapter, you will learn:

- ▶ How to configure a CloudFront distribution on the Amazon S3 bucket
- ▶ How to measure throughput between S3 and CloudFront
- ▶ How to compare costs for data transfer between S3 and CloudFront

Introduction

Amazon CloudFront CDN is a content delivery service that is used to speed up the distribution of your static and dynamic content, for example, `.html`, `.css`, `.php`, image files, and streaming media to the end users. CloudFront delivers your content stored in origin servers such as Amazon S3 bucket or web servers through global network data centers called edge locations all over the world. All you need to do is create a CloudFront distribution to define your origin server, cache behavior settings, and distribution settings, and store your content in the origin server, so that CloudFront distributes the configuration to CloudFront edge locations and adds the cache in the edge locations.

When a user requests your content to be served with CloudFront, the user can get your content through the edge location that provides the lowest latency by routing the request to the nearest edge location. If the content is not distributed in the edge location, CloudFront retrieves your content from the origin server such as an Amazon S3 bucket or a web server you configured.

Refer to the following diagram to get a better understanding of the workflow of the Amazon S3 bucket as origin servers, CloudFront distribution, and CloudFront edge locations.

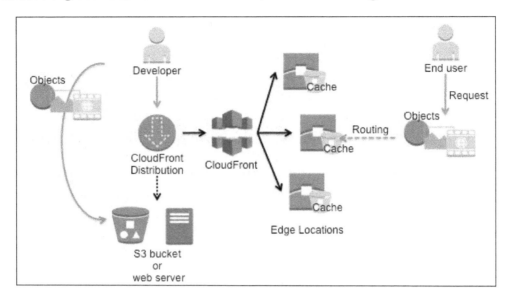

 The Amazon CloudFront global edge network is provided all over the world. Amazon CloudFront edge locations are located in the United States, Europe, Asia, South America, and Australia, and the total number of the edge locations is 51 locations so far. You can see more details about the edge locations at http://aws.amazon.com/cloudfront/details/.

How to configure a CloudFront distribution on the Amazon S3 bucket

To deliver your content in an Amazon S3 bucket through CloudFront edge locations, it is necessary to configure your bucket as an origin store by defining a CloudFront web distribution, specifying the S3 bucket as an origin server, and storing your content on the S3 bucket. After creating a CloudFront web distribution, the distribution will be available within the next 15 minutes. Then, they can receive the content through the closest edge location, not directly from the configured S3 bucket as an origin server. This is how CloudFront speeds up distribution of your content and minimizes network latency through the edge locations.

Getting ready

You do not have to request or fill-in any forms or pay any initial cost to use Amazon CloudFront CDN. All you need to do is to:

- ▸ Sign up for the AWS management console and access the Amazon CloudFront CDN using your IAM credentials
- ▸ Prepare your Amazon S3 bucket as an origin server to store your content

How to do it...

Let's follow these steps to deliver your content through CloudFront edge locations so that we can configure a web distribution, define parameters for the distribution, and finally confirm that your content on the S3 bucket is cached and delivered through the CloudFront edge locations all over the world:

1. Sign in to the AWS management console and move to the CloudFront console at `https://console.aws.amazon.com/cloudfront`.
2. Click on the **Create Distribution** button.

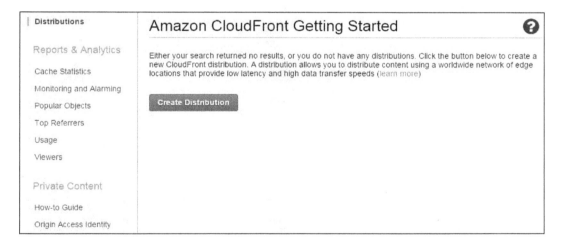

3. There are two delivery methods in the original CloudFront to create a distribution. In the **Step 1: Select a delivery method for your content** section, click on **Get Started**:

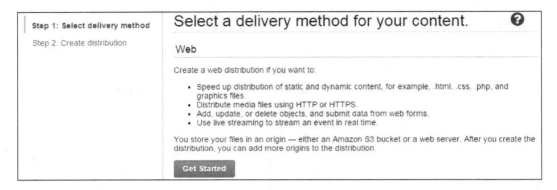

4. As shown in the following screenshot, fill in each parameters at each section and click on **Create Distribution**:

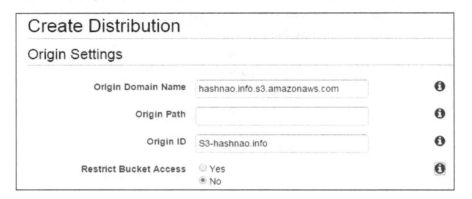

Let's discuss each parameters in detail:

- ► **Origin Settings**: In the **Origin Domain Name** field, select the Amazon S3 bucket that you want to configure as an origin server. Use the default value in the **Origin ID** box and the **Restrict Bucket Access** box. The reason to use the default value is that it is much easier to quickly evaluate CloudFront without any change.

- ► **Default Cache Behavior Settings**: Use the default value in the **Default Cache Behavior Settings** section. The default settings behave as follows:

  - ❑ **Path Pattern**: This forwards all the requests that use the CloudFront URL for your distribution to your S3 bucket configured as your origin in the **Origin Settings** section.

  - ❑ **Viewer Protocol Policy**: This allows end users to use either HTTP or HTTPS to access your content.

- **Allowed HTTP Methods**: This responds to requests for your content.
- **Forward Headers**: This chooses the options to cache objects to your origin based on request headers.
- **Object Caching**: This caches your content at the CloudFront edge locations for 24 hours.
- **Object Caching**: This is the cache-control header to control how long your objects stay in the CloudFront cache is added to your origin server. If you want to control the minimum time for your objects in the CloudFront cache, choose **Customize** and specify Minimum TTL in the **Minimum TTL** box.
- **Forward Cookies / Forward Query Settings**: All user cookies in the request URLs do not forward all of your cookies to your origin server.
- **Smooth Streaming**: This value helps you decide whether to use the Microsoft Smooth Streaming protocol for on-demand streaming. Choose **No**, if you are not planning to use the Microsoft Smooth Streaming format.
- **Restrict Viewer Access**: This value helps you decide whether to access your content using a sighed URL such as for a private content. Choose **No**, if you are planning to allow everyone to access your content.

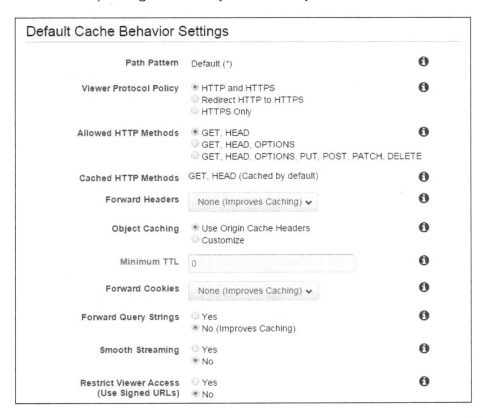

If you want to change the values of the default cache behavior settings, you can check this link for further information `http://docs.aws.amazon.com/AmazonCloudFront/latest/DeveloperGuide/distribution-web-values-specify.html#DownloadDistValuesCacheBehavior`.

▸ **Distribution Settings**: Enter the following applicable values for each setting:

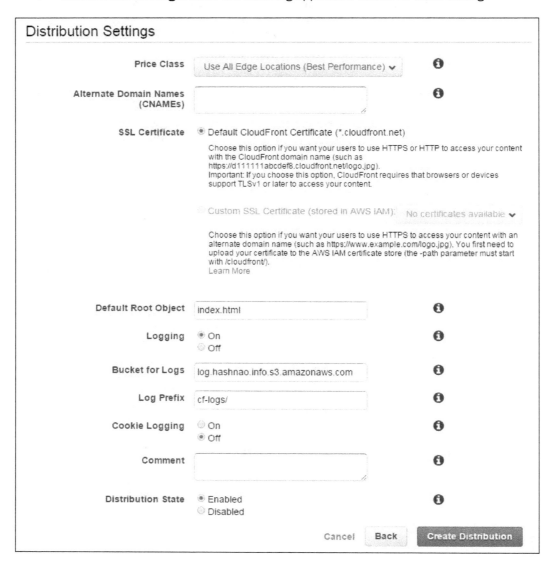

- **Price Class**: Choose the price class between **Use Only US and Europe, Use Only US, Europe and Asia**, and **Use All Edge Locations (Best Performance)**. If you want to lower your cost, you can choose a class other than **Use All Edge Locations (Best Performance)**. However, the latency might be longer for the users out of the regions you specified.

> We will cover the Amazon CloudFront pricing later, but you can see further details about the pricing model at `http://aws.amazon.com/cloudfront/pricing/`.

- **Alternate Domain Names (CNAMEs)**: This setting is optional. If you want to use your own domain name, then specify your CNAME for the CloudFront distribution name. For example, you need to create a CNAME record such as `www.example.com` with your DNS service in advance, in order to route queries from `d1234.cloudfront.net` to your CNAME. When you create a distribution, CloudFront will generate the distribution domain name.

> If you are planning to use your own domain for your CloudFront distribution, then go through `http://docs.aws.amazon.com/AmazonCloudFront/latest/DeveloperGuide/CNAMEs.html`.

- **SSL Certificate**: Choose **DefaultCloudFrontCertificate (*.cloudfront.net)** if you want your end users to access your content with the CloudFront domain name, such as `https://d11234.cloudfront.net/`. Otherwise, you can upload and choose your custom SSL certificate if you want to use your own domain name and custom SSL certificate with extra charges.

> We will not cover Amazon CloudFront Custom SSL here, however, you can check it out because it is necessary to pay an additional cost to use this function. For more information, see `http://aws.amazon.com/cloudfront/custom-ssl-domains/`.

- **Default Root Object**: This setting is optional. For example, if you define a default object URL as `index.html`, CloudFront replies to your root URL such as (`http://www.example.com`) instead of specifying the object URL. Enter only your object file name, such as `index.php` or `index.html` and not `/index.php` or `/index.html`.

The file can be of any type supported by CloudFront. You can also see a list of constraints on the file name at `http://docs.aws.amazon.com/AmazonCloudFront/latest/APIReference/DistributionConfigDatatype.html`.

- **Logging**: This setting is optional. Choose whether you want CloudFront to record access for your distribution. If you enable **Logging**, you also need to specify the bucket name and the log prefix.

- **Bucket for Logs**: This setting is also optional. If you enable logging, click on the field and enter the S3 bucket name that you want to save the web access logs as.

- **Log Prefix**: This setting is optional. If you enable logging, click on the field and enter the names of log files.

- **Cookie Logging**: If you enable cookie logging, CloudFront logs the cookies in all requests.

- **Comment**: This setting is optional. Add your comment about the distribution.

- **Distribution State**: If the distribution is enabled, CloudFront processes and accepts the requests from the viewers for the content associated with this distribution. If not, CloudFront does not accept any requests for the associated.

As shown in the following screenshot, a CloudFront distribution is being processed and the status will be **In Progress**:

 It takes less than 15 minutes to change the status from **In Progress** to **Deployed**.

How it works...

After CloudFront has created your distribution and the status column for the distribution becomes **Deployed**, the distribution will be ready to process requests. CloudFront knows where your S3 bucket is and generates the domain name for the distribution:

1. Check the domain name for the distribution at the **Domain Name** column. As shown in the following screenshot, you can see your domain name (the domain name generated for my distribution is **lsd1euruj0mgmg9b.cloudfront.net**).

2. Open your browser and type the domain name, and you can access the domain with both HTTP and HTTPS.

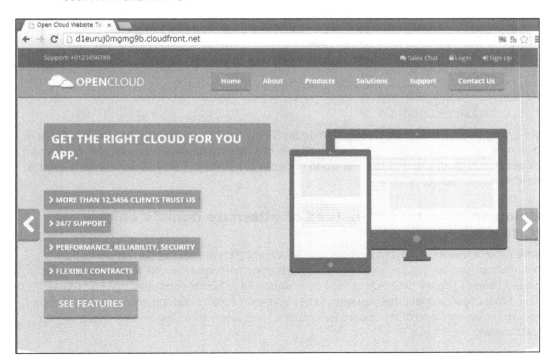

3. When you use the `dig` command and lookup the domain name for distribution, you can see that the domain name returns several global IP addresses and they are CloudFront Edge locations all over the world:

    The following output shows the result of looking up the domain name for the distribution using the dig command. The IP addresses could be different from the following output when you search the record because CloudFront automatically routes requests for the content:

    ```
    $ dig d1euruj0mgmg9b.cloudfront.net

    ;; QUESTION SECTION:
    ;d1euruj0mgmg9b.cloudfront.net.  IN       A

    ;; ANSWER SECTION:
    d1euruj0mgmg9b.cloudfront.net.  60 IN     A       216.137.52.123
    d1euruj0mgmg9b.cloudfront.net.  60 IN     A       216.137.52.245
    d1euruj0mgmg9b.cloudfront.net.  60 IN     A       54.230.108.71
    d1euruj0mgmg9b.cloudfront.net.  60 IN     A       54.230.110.129
    d1euruj0mgmg9b.cloudfront.net.  60 IN     A       54.230.110.146
    d1euruj0mgmg9b.cloudfront.net.  60 IN     A       54.230.111.31
    d1euruj0mgmg9b.cloudfront.net.  60 IN     A       54.230.111.159
    d1euruj0mgmg9b.cloudfront.net.  60 IN     A       54.230.111.239
    ```

> You can see the Amazon CloudFront Edge servers' IP ranges at https://forums.aws.amazon.com/ann.jspa?annID=2051. You need to login to the AWS console to see the content.

There's more...

We configured a CloudFront distribution on an S3 bucket and confirmed that the distribution becomes deployed and the website is available through the domain name for the distribution. However, it is insufficient in the real world because the domain name randomly generated is hard to remember for anyone.

Using an alias record instead of alternate domain names (CNAMEs)

When you create a CloudFront distribution, CloudFront generates a domain name for the distribution such as `d111111abcdef8.cloudfront.net` and the URL for an object called `/path/image.jpg` will be `http://d111111abcdef8.cloudfront.net/path/image.jpg`. Most of you will feel that you want to use your own custom domain name such as `image.exmaple.com` instead of the `xxx.cloudfront.net` name that CloudFront assigns to your distribution.

You can choose to use an alias record or CNAME to a domain name of your distribution with Route 53 as a DNS service. Here, we will use an alias record other than CNAME because Amazon Route 53 doesn't charge for alias queries to the CloudFront distribution and you do not need to pay for the queries.

 For more information, see `http://docs.aws.amazon.com/Route53/latest/DeveloperGuide/resource-record-sets-choosing-alias-non-alias.html`.

Let's see how to configure an alias record for the CloudFront distribution with Amazon Route 53:

1. Sign in to the AWS management console and move to the Route 53 console at `https://console.aws.amazon.com/route53`.

2. In the **Dashboard** section on the left-hand side, click on **Hosted Zones**:

3. Check the **Domain Name** box in which you want to create an alias record and click on **Go to Record Sets**:

4. As shown in the following screenshot, click on **Create Record Set**:

5. Enter the following applicable values for each setting and click on **Create**:
   - In the **Name** box, enter your record name
   - In the **Type** box, use the default value, **A – IPv4 address**
   - In the **Alias** box, choose **Yes**
   - In the **Alias Target** box, enter the CloudFront domain name for your distribution

6. Move the CloudFront console, check the distribution, and click on **Distribution Settings**:

7. In the **General** tab, click on **Edit**:

8. In the **Alternate Domain Names (CNAMEs)** box, enter the alias record name, and click on **Yes, Edit**:

9. As shown in the following screenshot, open your browser and type the alias record to access the URL:

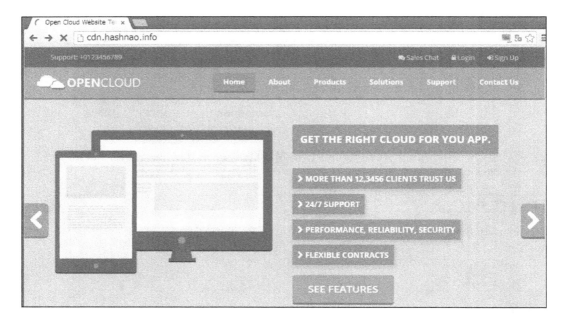

 If you want to use an alternate domain name and HTTPS at the same time, you need to consider SNI Custom SSL or Dedicated IP Custom SSL. For more information, see `https://aws.amazon.com/cloudfront/custom-ssl-domains/`.

See also

▶ *What is Amazon CloudFront?* `http://docs.aws.amazon.com/AmazonCloudFront/latest/DeveloperGuide/Introduction.html`

▶ *Amazon CloudFront Troubleshooting* `http://docs.aws.amazon.com/AmazonCloudFront/latest/DeveloperGuide/Troubleshooting.html`

How to measure throughput between S3 and CloudFront

As we configured a CloudFront distribution on the Amazon S3 bucket, we also need to know how the latency between S3 and CloudFront differs.

In the Amazon CloudFront official document, it says:

"Traditional load testing methods don't work well with CloudFront because CloudFront uses DNS to balance loads across geographically dispersed edge locations and within each edge location."

 If you seriously need to plan a load testing on CloudFront edge locations, you might want to see this document `http://docs.aws.amazon.com/AmazonCloudFront/latest/DeveloperGuide/load-testing.html`.

Getting ready

We will be using a load test site called **LOAD IMPACT** (`https://loadimpact.com/`) to process a load testing because it is free and can be used quickly. Also, it is not necessary to prepare tens of load test servers that need to be geographically separated all over the world and install load test tools (such as ApacheBench, Apache JMeter, Curl-loader, or Httperf).

 LOAD IMPACT also provides monthly subscriptions based on the number of max concurrent users or test duration. For more information, see `https://loadimpact.com/pricing`.

How to do it...

We will be processing the load test for a S3 static website endpoint and the CloudFront edge locations that are defined in the S3 bucket as an origin server. The scenarios for both endpoints are as follows:

Edit test configuration		
Test configuration name	S3	CloudFront
Target URL	`http://hashnao.info.s3-website-ap-northeast-1.amazonaws.com/`	`http://cdn.hashnao.info/`

Load test execution plan			
	Max VUs	250	250
	Duration (Min)	5	5
User scenarios			
	Allocation percent	34 percent	34 percent
	Load zone	Ashburn, US (Amazon)	Ashburn, US (Amazon)
	Allocation percent	33 percent	33 percent
	Load zone	Singapore, SG (Amazon)	Singapore, SG (Amazon)
	Allocation percent	33 percent	33 percent
	Load zone	Sydney, AU (Amazon)	Sydney, AU (Amazon)

Let's see how to create a test configuration and process the load testing step by step:

1. Open your browser, and type `http://loadimpact.com/`. Sign in to the LOAD IMPACT. Your screen will look something like this:

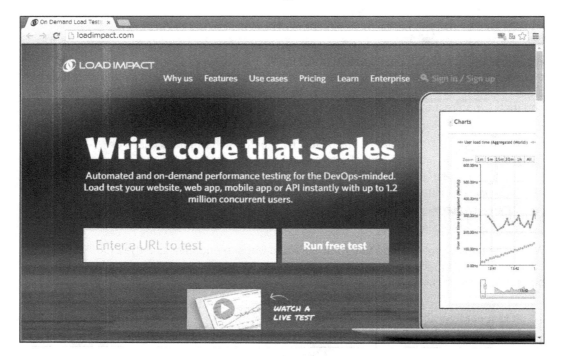

[LOAD IMPACT can be used without creating an account (as a run free test). The reason why I created my account is to create a test configuration, and to choose and define several conditions and parameters for load testing.]

2. As shown in the following screenshot, create a test configuration by configuring the following parameters:

    ❏ **Edit test configuration**: In the **Test configuration name** box, specify your configuration name. In the **Target URL** box, specify the URL to process a load test:

    ❏ **Load test execution plan**: In the **Max VUs (Virtual User)** box, enter the number of concurrent users. In the **Duration (Min)** box, enter how many minutes you want to process a load test:

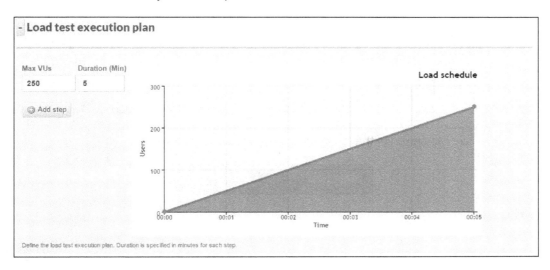

- **User scenarios**: In the **Allocation** % box, specify the ratio to allocate. In the **Load zone** box, select the location. If you want to add a scenario, click on **Add scenario**:

- Skip the following settings and click on **Save test configuration and start test**:

- As shown in the following screenshot, click on **Start test**:

3. As shown in the following screenshot, the **Status** column shows **Test finished** after the test has been finished:

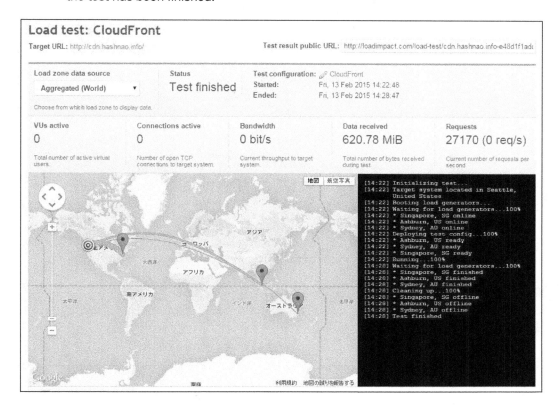

 LOAD IMPACT generates a Test result public URL after finishing your load test.

How it works...

After finishing the load test, LOAD IMPACT generates the summary, charts, pages, URLs, and the logs section. Let's see the chart section for both the S3 and CloudFront test result, and compare both the user load time.

The following graphs show the average time that aggregates in the three load zone (Ashburn, US, Singapore, SG, and Sydney, AU):

▸ On S3:

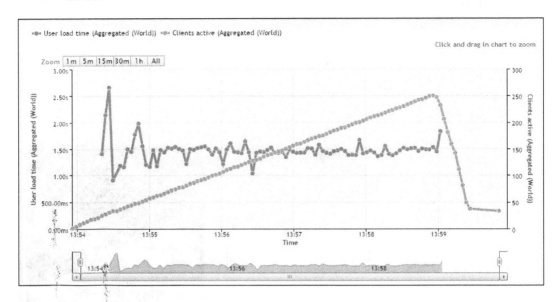

▸ On CloudFront:

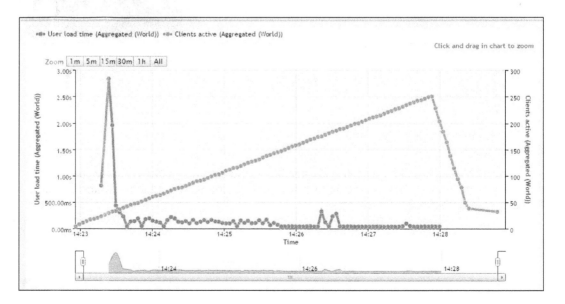

It is clear that the result of CloudFront is much faster than that of S3 because the load time via CloudFront is always less than 500 milliseconds, while the load time of S3 is around 1.5 seconds.

Let's see another chart that shows the user load time for each load zone to break down.

- On S3:

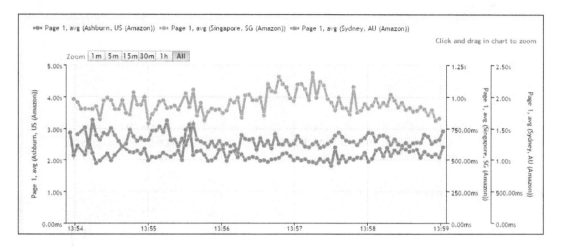

- On CloudFront:

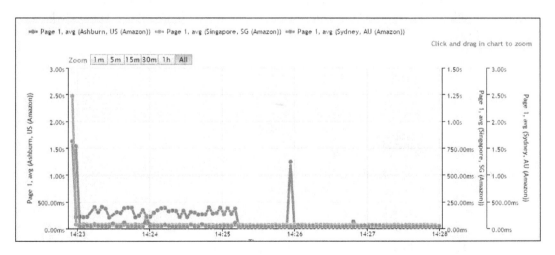

In the load time of CloudFront, the graph from Ashburn, US is travelling between 250 milliseconds back and forth and the rest of the load zone (Singapore, SG and Sydney, AU) is stable and always less than 50 milliseconds.

Of course, it is much more complex and tiresome to process a load testing and measure the performance of a website in the real world. However, it will indicate how much the response or the load time differs by comparing the load time between Amazon S3 bucket and CloudFront edge locations.

The test result public URLs for both, the S3 and CloudFront load tests, are available at:

- **S3**: `http://loadimpact.com/load-test/hashnao.info.s3-website-ap-northeast-1.amazonaws.com-c80f05e1372173624e9953342e0df72f`

- **CloudFront**: `http://loadimpact.com/load-test/cdn.hashnao.info-e48d1f1add35cfa2619457ccb2fb0b75`

There's more...

As you configured CloudFront distribution on your website, you may think that your website is endlessly scalable with the help of CloudFront edge locations across the world. However, you should remember AWS service limits exist.

Amazon CloudFront limits

Amazon CloudFront has limited its resources, by default, and is available at `http://docs.aws.amazon.com/general/latest/gr/aws_service_limits.html#limits_cloudfront`.

If you expect more than the default limit value for one of the resources (for example, you need more bandwidth for an event next week), you can create a case to request a higher limit via AWS Support Dashboard.

 For more information on how to request, see
`http://aws.amazon.com/cloudfront/faqs/`.

See also

- *Load Testing CloudFront* `http://docs.aws.amazon.com/AmazonCloudFront/latest/DeveloperGuide/load-testing.html`

- *Amazon CloudFront Limits* `http://docs.aws.amazon.com/general/latest/gr/aws_service_limits.html#limits_cloudfront`

- *LOAD IMPACT Features* `https://loadimpact.com/features`

How to compare costs for data transfer between S3 and CloudFront

In *Chapter 3, Calculating Cost with AWS Simple Monthly Calculator*, you learned about the S3 pricing model and how to calculate S3 cost including Storage, Request, and Data Transfer pricing and CloudFront with the AWS calculator. This section looks into the details of the CloudFront pricing model by comparing costs for data transferring.

Getting ready

The CloudFront pricing model is composed of Regional Data Transfer Out to Internet, Regional Data Transfer Out to Origin, and Request Pricing for All HTTP methods. Let's see the details of each model one by one.

> See the latest pricing table at `http://aws.amazon.com/cloudfront/pricing/`.

Regional data transfer out to the Internet (per GB)

The data volume transferred out of the Amazon CloudFront edge locations to the Internet is separately measured for each geographic region in GB. There is a volume discount shown in the table above as the data transferred increases.

Let's assume that you transfer 1 TB of data out of the CloudFront edge locations in the United States to the Internet every day for a 31-day month. The Regional Data Transfer Out to Internet pricing will be calculated as follows:

- ▸ *10 TB Tier: 10,240 GB (10 * 1024 GB/TB) * $0.085 = $870.40*
- ▸ *10 TB to 50 TB Tier: 21,504 GB (21 * 1024 GB/TB) * $0.080 = $1,720.32*

The total data transfer fee will be as follows:

- ▸ *$870.40 + $1,720.32 = $2,590.72*

Regional data transfer out to origin (per GB)

The data volume transferred out of the Amazon CloudFront edge locations to your origin such as web servers or Amazon S3 buckets is measured in GBs.

Let's assume that you transfer 100 GB of data out of the CloudFront edge locations in the United States to your origin every day for a 31-day month. The Regional Data Transfer Out to Origin pricing will be calculated as follows:

► The data volume transferred to your origin: *100 GB * 31 days = 3,100 GB*

The Regional Data Transfer Out to Origin fee will be as follows:

► The data volume transferred to your origin: *3,100 GB * $0.020 = $62.00*

Request pricing for all HTTP methods

Request pricing is based on the number of HTTP/HTTPS requests made to Amazon CloudFront for your content.

Let's assume that you transfer 10,000 files into Amazon S3 buckets and transfer 20,000 files out of the CloudFront edge locations in the United States for 10,000 HTTP requests and 10,000 HTTPS requests each day during the month. The request pricing will be calculated as follows:

► Total HTTP requests: *10,000 requests * 31 days = 310,000 requests*

► Total HTTPS requests: *10,000 requests * 31 days = 310,000 requests*

The total request fee will be as follows:

► HTTP Requests: *310,000 requests * $0.008 = $2,325.00*. This is for Hong Kong, Philippines, S. Korea, Singapore, and Taiwan.

► HTTPS Requests: *310,000 requests * $0.010 = $3,100.00*. You have to contact AWS Sales and Business Development for this.

CloudFront provides On-Demand Pricing and Reserved Capacity Pricing. This book covers On-Demand Pricing to calculate the CloudFront charges. Reserved Capacity Pricing provides the option to commit to a minimum monthly usage level for 12 months or longer and in turn receive a discount. For more information, see the Reserved Capacity Pricing section at http://aws.amazon.com/cloudfront/pricing/.

How to do it...

Do you remember the second and third examples in *Chapter 3, Calculating Cost with the AWS Simple Monthly Calculator*? Let's get back to *Chapter 3, Calculating Cost with the AWS Simple Monthly Calculator* and take a look at the conditions and structures of the second and the third examples and compare the cost for data transferring between S3 and CloudFront.

Let's summarize the conditions, considering that we have 1,000,000 users and we need to do the following:

- **PUT requests (Uploads)**: 27,000,000 a month (*1,000,000 users * 30% * 3 times * 30 days = 27,000,000 requests*)

- **GET requests**: 150,000,000 a month (*1,000,000 users * 50% * 10 times * 30 days = 150,000,000 requests*)

- **Data transfer**: 1 MB per request

The second example – transferred out of an S3 bucket to the Internet

We have an S3 bucket composed of Storage and **Reduced Redundancy Storage** (**RRS**) containing media files and our users upload their contents into the bucket and retrieve the contents through the bucket.

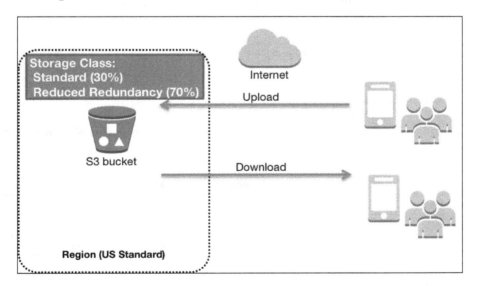

The third example – transferred out of CloudFront edge locations to the Internet

In the same environment as the second example, we have an S3 composed bucket of Storage and Reduced Redundancy Storage (RRS) containing media files and our users upload their contents into the bucket and retrieve the contents in the bucket through CloudFront distribution all over the world.

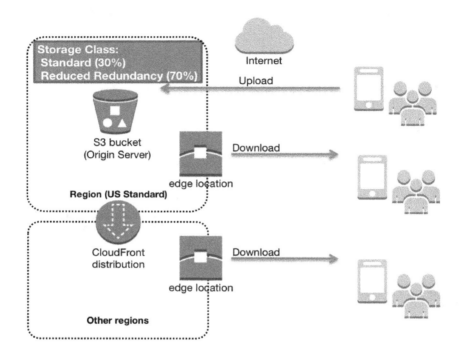

The following table shows the summary of the conditions for the examples (Parameters to be used for calculating):

			Second	Third	
Amazon S3					
	Storage				
		Storage	8,100	8,100	GB
		Reduced Redundancy Storage	18,900	18,900	GB
	Requests				
		PUT/COPY/POST/LIST Requests	27,000,000	27,000,000	Requests
		GET and Other Requests	150,000,000	0	Requests
	Data Transfer				

	Inter-Region Data Transfer Out	0	27,000	GB
	Data Transfer Out	150,000	0	GB
	Data Transfer In	27,000	27,000	GB
CloudFront				
	Data Transfer Out:			
	Monthly Volume	0	150,000	GB
Requests				
	Average Object Size	0	1,000	KB
	Type of Requests		HTTP	HTTP or HTTPS
	Invalidation Requests	0	0	Requests
Edge Location Traffic Distribution				
	United States	0	40	%
	Europe	0	10	%
	Hong Kong, Philippines, S. Korea, Singapore, and Taiwan	0	15	%
	Japan	0	20	%
	South America	0	0	%
	Australia	0	5	%
	India	0	10	%
Dedicated IP SSL Certificates				
	Number of Certificates	0	0	

The major difference between the second and third examples are as follows:

- **GET and Other Requests (Amazon S3)**: The second example includes 150,000,000 requests for GET and Other Requests because it transfers data out of the Amazon S3 bucket. The third has no request because it transfers data out of CloudFront edge locations.

- **Inter-Region Data Transfer Out (Amazon S3)**: The second example has no data for Inter-Region Data Transfer Out because it transfers data out of the Amazon S3 bucket. The third includes 27,000 GB because it transfers data out of CloudFront edge locations. The third example contains 27,000 GB for Inter-Region Data Transfer Out and the second one does not. This is because of CloudFront.

- **Data Transfer Out (Amazon S3)**: The second example includes 150,000 GB for Data Transfer Out because it transfers data out of the Amazon S3 bucket. The third has no data because it transfers data out of CloudFront edge locations.

▶ **Data Transfer Out (CloudFront)**: The second example has no data for Data Transfer Out because it transfers data out of the Amazon S3 bucket. The third includes 150,000 GB for Data Transfer Out because it transfers data out of CloudFront edge locations.

> If you are using an AWS origin (such as Amazon S3, Amazon EC2, and so on), Amazon CloudFront no longer charges for AWS data transfer out to CloudFront, which is effective as of December 1, 2014. This applies to data transfer from all AWS regions to all global CloudFront edge locations. Visit `http://aws.amazon.com/cloudfront/pricing/`.

How it works...

As you learned how to simulate S3 and CloudFront pricing, we will examine the difference for the fee between the data transfer out of the Amazon S3 bucket and CloudFront edge locations. The following table shows the overall IT costs for each example using the AWS calculator:

		Second		Third
Amazon S3 Service (US-East)		881		1,361
Storage	239		239	
Reduced Redundancy Storage:	446		446	
Put/List Requests	135		135	
GET and Other Requests	60		0	
Inter-Region Data Transfer Out	0		540	
Amazon CloudFront Service		0		18,934
Data Transfer Out	0		18,802	
Requests	0		132	
AWS Data Transfer In		0		0
US-East / US Standard (Virginia) Region	0		0	
AWS Data Transfer Out		11,319		0
US-East / US Standard (Virginia) Region	11,319		0	
Total Monthly Payment	**$12,200**		**$20,295**	

The major difference between the second the third examples are as follows:

▶ **Data Transfer Out (Amazon CloudFront)**: The third includes $18,802 for Data Transfer Out because it transfers data out of CloudFront edge locations. The Regional Data Transfer Out to Internet price differs by regions shown in the *How to configure a CloudFront distribution on Amazon S3 bucket* section.

See also

- ▶ *CloudFront Billing and Usage Reports* `http://docs.aws.amazon.com/AmazonCloudFront/latest/DeveloperGuide/reports.html`
- ▶ *Choosing the Price Class for a CloudFront Distribution* `http://docs.aws.amazon.com/AmazonCloudFront/latest/DeveloperGuide/PriceClass.html`

6

Securing Resources with Bucket Policies and IAM

This chapter is divided into two parts; the first part is an introduction to the access control method and the difference between resource-based policies and user policies, and the last part includes bucket policy examples and their structures based on common use cases with the following walkthroughs:

- ▶ Walkthrough 1: To grant users bucket permissions
- ▶ Walkthrough 2: To grant cross-account bucket permissions
- ▶ Walkthrough 3: To grant cross-account bucket permissions to objects without ownership
- ▶ Walkthrough 4: Bucket and user policy examples

Introduction

Amazon S3 resources consist of buckets, objects, and related subresources (such as the website configuration that we used to create a static website or logging configuration that we used for storing S3 access logging) are private. To manage access permissions to your Amazon S3 resources, it is necessary to understand that Amazon S3 provides access policy options which are mainly categorized into resource-based policies and user polices. For example, bucket polices and **access control lists** (**ACLs**) are defined as resource-based polices because the access polices can be attached to your resources such as buckets and objects. On the other hand, you can attach the access policies to users in your AWS account and they are defined as user policies.

You can use resource-based polices or user polices or both of them at the same time to manage access to your S3 resources.

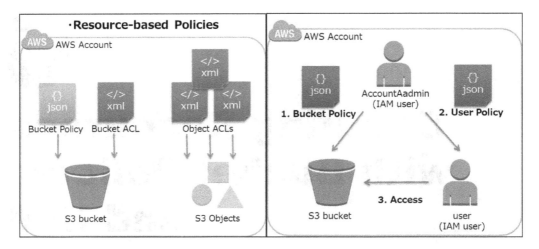

To be able to manage access to your buckets or objects using both bucket policies and user policies, it is necessary to understand how to configure access polices and how they work when the polices are applied based on the situations or conditions. We will be learning how to use bucket policies and user policies in the following *How to do it...* sections and the sample policy sections one by one.

Walkthrough 1: To grant users bucket permissions

The first walkthrough is that an AWS account owns a bucket and has an IAM user in the AWS account. The scenario is as follows:

▸ The IAM user has no permissions and needs to be granted permissions to operate any tasks on the bucket

▸ The bucket owner and the parent account are the same

▸ The AWS account can use a bucket policy, a user policy or both to grant its user permissions on the bucket

 AWS **IAM (Identification and Access Management)** is to control access to AWS resources. For more information about IAM, see http://docs.aws.amazon.com/IAM/latest/UserGuide/introduction.html.

The following diagram shows the relation between an AWS account, an S3 bucket, an IAM user, a bucket policy, and a user policy for this walkthrough:

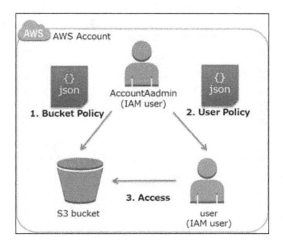

To summarize, what you need to do is:

1. Create a bucket policy with a set of permissions for the IAM user.
2. Attach a user policy to the IAM user with additional permissions.
3. Verify that the IAM user is granted permissions via both the bucket policy and the user policy.

We refer to the AWS account ID, the AWS account, and the administrator user as follows:

AWS Account ID	Account Referred to as	Administrator user in the account
1111-1111-1111	Account A	AccountAadmin

Getting ready

All the operations to create an IAM user and grant permissions are performed through the management console. To verify the permissions, we use AWS CLI. All you need to do is:

▸ Create Account A with the administrator policy instead of using the root credentials of the AWS account

 To create an IAM administrator user, see `http://docs.aws.amazon.com/AmazonS3/latest/dev/example-walkthroughs-managing-access.html#about-using-root-credentials`.

▶ Install and set up AWS CLI in your PC or use Amazon Linux AMI

 For more information about how to set up AWS CLI, see `http://docs.aws.amazon.com/AmazonS3/latest/dev/policy-eval-walkthrough-download-awscli.html`. AWS Tools for Windows PowerShell can be also used for verifying the permissions.

How to do it...

First, we sign up to the management console using the Account A credentials, move to the IAM management console, and then create an IAM user `AccountAadmin` and grant administrator permissions with full access to the IAM user.

Next, sign up to the management console using the AccountAadmin credentials, create a bucket and an IAM user called Tom (who can access only the bucket) and grant permissions by attaching a bucket policy to the bucket and a user policy to the IAM user.

Lastly, we verify that the permissions work (using the credentials from Tom) by uploading a sample object into the bucket with AWS CLI.

The first step is to create an IAM user referred as `AccountAadmin` in Account A and grant permissions:

1. Sign in to the AWS management console using the Account A credentials and move to the IAM console at `https://console.aws.amazon.com/iam/`.

2. Click on **Users**, and then click on **Create New Users** as shown in the following screenshot:

3. In the **Enter User Names** box, enter `AccountAadmin`, disable the **Generate an access key for each user** box, and click on **Create**:

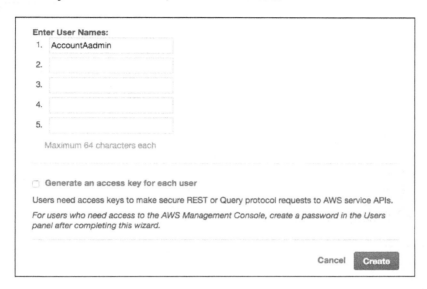

4. Then, click on **AccountAadmin** as shown in the following screenshot:

5. In the **Permission** section, click on **Attach Policy**:

6.   Enable the **AdministartorAccess** checkbox and click on **Attach Policy**:

7.   In the **Security Credentials** section, click on the **Manage Password** button:

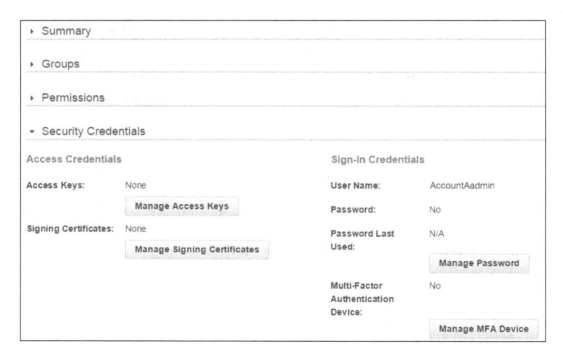

8. Use **Assign an auto-generated password** and then click on the **Apply** button:

9. Click on **Show User Security Credentials** or click on the **Download Credentials** button and retrieve your credentials:

We have created an administrator user referred and will now create a bucket and an IAM user, and attach a bucket policy to the bucket.

The second step is to create a bucket, attach a bucket policy to the bucket, create an IAM user, and attach `https://console.aws.amazon.com/s3/` called Tom to operate the S3 bucket following the instruction in *the first step...* and note down the credentials.

> We do not need to create and attach an IAM policy to the IAM user, just create an IAM user and issue credentials.

1. In the Amazon S3 console, check the bucket name you created. In the **Permissions** section, click on **Add bucket policy**:

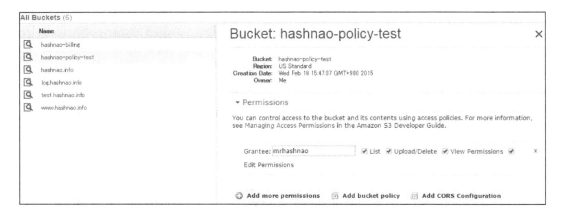

2. Attach the following bucket policy and click on **Save** as shown in the following screenshot:

- ❑ AccountA-ID is to be replaced with your AWS account ID
- ❑ IAMUserName is to be replaced with the IAM user name

❑ `S3BucketName` is to be replaced with the bucket name

```
{
  "Version": "2012-10-17",
  "Statement": [
    {
      "Sid": "ListGet",
      "Effect": "Allow",
      "Principal": {
        "AWS": "arn:aws:iam::AccountA-ID:user/IAMUserName"
      },
      "Action": [
        "s3:GetBucketLocation",
        "s3:ListBucket"
      ],
      "Resource": [
        "arn:aws:s3:::S3BucketName"
      ]
    },
    {
      "Sid": "GetObject",
      "Effect": "Allow",
      "Principal": {
        "AWS": "arn:aws:iam::AccountA-ID:user/IAMUserName "
      },
      "Action": [
        "s3:GetObject"
      ],
      "Resource": [
        "arn:aws:s3:::S3BucketName/*"
      ]
    }
  ]
}
```

3. In the IAM console, click on **Users**, and then click on the IAM user:

4. In the **Permissions** section, click on **Inline Policies** and then on **click here**:

5. Select **Custom Policy** and then, click on the **Select** button:

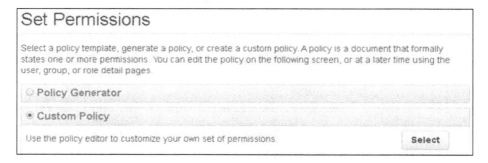

6. Attach the following user policy and click on the **Apply Policy** button:

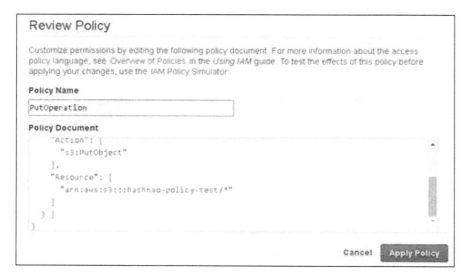

S3BucketName is to be replaced with the bucket name, as follows:

```
{
    "Version": "2012-10-17",
    "Statement": [
        {
            "Sid": "PermissionForObjectOperations",
            "Effect": "Allow",
            "Action": [
                "s3:PutObject"
            ],
            "Resource": [
                "arn:aws:s3:::S3BucketName/*"
            ]
        }
    ]
}
```

How it works...

As we finished configuring the bucket policy on the bucket and the user policy on the IAM user, let's see how they work using AWS CLI to verify the permissions. First, we create the AWS CLI config file for the IAM user to operate the bucket, and then verify that the permissions granted in the user policy have been applied with AWS CLI and the credentials:

1. Update the AWS config file entering the IAM credentials:

```
$ vim ~/.aws/config
[profile UserTom]
aws_access_key_id = access-key
aws_secret_access_key = secret-access-key
region = us-east-1
```

2. Verify that the IAM user can upload an object using AWS CLI, as follows:

```
$ bucket=your-bucket-name
$ profile=UserTom
$ object=policy_test.txt
$ aws s3api put-object --bucket ${bucket}
--key ${object} --body ${object} \
--profile ${profile}
{
    "ETag": "\"d41d8cd98f00b204e9800998ecf8427e\""
}
```

3. Verify that the IAM user can retrieve an object in the bucket using AWS CLI, as follows:

```
$ aws s3api get-object --bucket ${bucket} \
--key ${object} output_file.txt \
--profile ${profile}
{
    "AcceptRanges": "bytes",
    "ContentType": "binary/octet-stream",
    "LastModified": "Thu, 19 Feb 2015 00:35:26 GMT",
    "ContentLength": "0",
    "ETag": "\"d41d8cd98f00b204e9800998ecf8427e\""
}
```

4. Verify and check whether the IAM user is allowed to perform only the operations defined in the user policy using AWS CLI, as follows:

```
$ bucket=other-bucket

$ aws s3api put-object --bucket ${bucket} \
--key ${object} --body ${object} \
--profile ${profile}
A client error (PermanentRedirect) occurred when calling the
PutObject operation: The bucket you are attempting to access
must be addressed using the specified endpoint. Please send
all future requests to this endpoint.
```

As shown in the preceding error message, you can see that the IAM user fails to upload an object to the other bucket that is not defined in the user policy:

```
$ aws s3 ls --profile ${profile}
A client error (AccessDenied) occurred when calling the ListBuckets
operation: Access Denied
```

In addition, as shown in the preceding error message, you can see that the IAM user fails to list the entire bucket and is allowed to list only the bucket defined in the user policy.

Finally, let's examine each element in the bucket policy and the user policy again so that we can understand how the elements in the bucket and user policies function with each other.

The bucket policy

The `Principal` element defines the IAM user in the AWS account is allowed to grant the permissions in the `Action` element. The actions granted are `s3:GetBucketLocation` and `s3:ListBucket`:

```
"Principal": {
  "AWS": "arn:aws:iam::AccountA-ID:user/IAMUserName"
},
"Action": [
```

```
    "s3:GetBucketLocation",
    "s3:ListBucket"
  ],
```

The `Resource` element defines whether the S3 bucket is allowed to be performed. The IAM user can get the bucket location such as us-east-1 or us-west-1, and list buckets but only the bucket defined in the `Resource` element:

```
"Resource": [
  "arn:aws:s3:::S3BucketName"
] }, {
```

We also have `Principal` and `Action` elements. The actions granted is `s3:GetObject`. The same IAM user can get objects but only the objects in the bucket that are defined in the `Resource` element:

```
"Principal": {
  "AWS": "arn:aws:iam::AccountA-ID:user/IAMUserName "
},
"Action": [
  "s3:GetObject"
],
"Resource": [
  "arn:aws:s3:::S3BucketName/*"
]
```

The user policy

The user policy is applied for the IAM user, Tom, and the policy grants `s3:PutObject`. Tom can put objects, but only the objects that are defined in the `Resource` element:

```
"Action": [
  "s3:PutObject"
],
"Resource": [
  "arn:aws:s3:::S3BucketName/*"
]
```

See also

▶ *Example 1: Bucket Owner Granting Its Users Bucket Permissions* `http://docs.aws.amazon.com/AmazonS3/latest/dev/example-walkthroughs-managing-access-example1.html`

▶ *How Amazon S3 Authorizes a Request for a Bucket Operation* `http://docs.aws.amazon.com/AmazonS3/latest/dev/access-control-auth-workflow-bucket-operation.html`

▸ *Guidelines for Using the Available Access Policy Options* http://docs.aws.amazon.com/AmazonS3/latest/dev/access-policy-alternatives-guidelines.html

Walkthrough 2: To grant cross-account bucket permissions

If you own several AWS accounts (for example, Account A and Account B for different projects) and grant permissions to access the resources such as buckets or objects between the accounts, for example, you want to grant permissions that Account A allows Account B to access the objects or buckets of Account A, you can grant such permissions using cross-account permissions.

The following diagram shows how the AWS account A grants permissions to the S3 bucket, and the Admin IAM user in the AWS account B delegates permission to a different IAM user in its account and for this walkthrough.

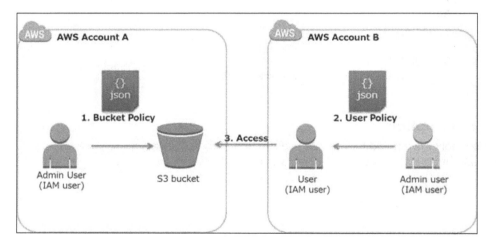

To summarize, what you need to do is:

1. Create a bucket policy in Account A, granting cross-account permission to Account B to perform specific operations.

2. Attach a user policy in Account B to the IAM user to delegate permissions from Account A.

3. Verify that the IAM user in Account B is granted permissions to access objects in the bucket owned by Account A.

We refer to the AWS account ID, the AWS account, and the administrator user as follows:

AWS Account ID	Account Referred to as	Administrator user in the account
1111-1111-1111	Account A	AccountAadmin
2222-2222-2222	Account B	AccountBadmin

Getting ready

All you need to do is follow the same steps showed in the *Walkthrough 1: To grant users bucket permissions* recipe.

How to do it...

First, we create a bucket and attach a bucket policy to the bucket in Account A to grant cross-account permissions to Account B, and then verify that Account B can perform the operations using AccountBadmin credentials.

Next, we create an IAM user called Dan in Account B and delegate permissions to the IAM user.

Lastly, verify that the permissions work using the credentials from Dan by uploading a sample object into the bucket owned by Account A with AWS CLI.

The first step is to create a bucket and an IAM user, attach a bucket policy in Account A, and verify that Account B can perform the operations using the AccountBadmin credentials:

1. Sign in to the AWS management console using the AccountAadmin credentials and move to the S3 console at `https://console.aws.amazon.com/s3/`.

2. Attach the following bucket policy to the bucket you created by following the instructions at *Walkthrough 1: To grant users bucket permissions*:

   ❑ `AccountB-ID` is to be replaced with AWS Account B ID

   ❑ `S3BucketName` is to be replaced with the Bucket name:

   ```
   {
       "Version": "2012-10-17",
       "Statement": [
         {
           "Sid": "AccpuntBPermissions",
           "Effect": "Allow",
           "Principal": {
             "AWS": "arn:aws:iam::AccountB-ID:root"
           },
           "Action": [
   ```

```
        "s3:GetBucketLocation",
        "s3:ListBucket"
      ],
      "Resource": [
        "arn:aws:s3:::S3BucketName"
      ]
    }
  ]
}
```

3. Update the AWS config file of Account B credentials by entering its IAM credentials:

```
$ vim ~/.aws/config
[profile AccountBadmin]
aws_access_key_id = access-key
aws_secret_access_key = secret-access-key
region = us-east-1
```

4. Verify that AccountBadmin can list the bucket:

```
$ bucket=your-bucket-name"
$ profile=AccountBadmin
$ aws s3 ls s3://${bucket} --profile ${profile}
2015-02-19 09:35:26          0 policy_test.txt
```

5. Verify that AccountBadmin can get the bucket location:

```
$ aws s3api get-bucket-location --bucket ${bucket} --profile
${profile}
{
    "LocationConstraint": null
}
```

The second step is to create an IAM user called Dan in Account B, delegate permission to the IAM user, and then verify the IAM user can perform operations:

1. Sign in to the AWS management console using the AccountBadmin credentials and move it to the IAM console at https://console.aws.amazon.com/iam/.

2. Create an IAM user Dan following the instructions in *the first step...* and make a note of the credentials.

3. Attach the following user policy to Dan following the instructions at *Walkthrough 1: To grant users bucket permissions*:

S3BucketName is to be replaced with the Bucket name:

```
{
  "Version": "2012-10-17",
  "Statement": [
    {
```

```
          "Sid": "ListBucket",
          "Effect": "Allow",
          "Action": [
            "s3:ListBucket"
          ],
          "Resource": [
            "arn:aws:s3:::S3BucketName"
          ]
        }
      ]
    }
```

How it works...

Let's see how they work using AWS CLI to verify the permissions. First, we update the AWS CLI config file for Dan to list the bucket, and then verify the cross-account permissions to verify that Dan can list the bucket granted in the user policy with AWS CLI using the credentials from Dan:

1. Update the credentials of Dan in the AWS config file entering its IAM credentials:

```
$ vim ~/.aws/config
[profile UserDan]
aws_access_key_id = access-key
aws_secret_access_key = secret-access-key
region = us-east-1
```

2. Verify that Dan can list the bucket:

```
$ bucket=your-bucket-name
$ profile=UserDan
$ aws s3 ls s3://${bucket} --profile ${profile}
2015-02-20 12:49:51            0 policy_test.txt
```

Finally, let's examine each element in the bucket policy and the user policy again so that we can understand how the bucket and user policy work to grant cross-account permissions.

The bucket policy

The difference between walkthrough 1 and 2 is that AWS Account B (ID) is defined in the `Principal` element. The reason is because it is necessary that Account B delegates the permissions from Dan received from Account A:

```
          "Principal": {
            "AWS": "arn:aws:iam::AccountB-ID:root"
          },
              "AWS": "arn:aws:iam::AccountA-ID:user/IAMUserName"
```

The user policy

The user policy is much simpler because it just needs to define the `Action` element and the `Resource` element. The policy grants `s3:ListObject` in the `Action` element and specifies the resource referred as `S3BucketName` in the `Resource` element:

```
"Action": [
  "s3:ListBucket"
],
"Resource": [
  "arn:jaws:s3:::S3BucketName"
]
```

For the following user policy, Dan can list the bucket but cannot perform any other operations. For example, the following command (such as `get-bucket-location` or `get-object`) fails because it is not allowed in the user policy using credentials from Dan:

```
$ aws s3api get-bucket-location --bucket ${bucket} \
--profile ${profile}
A client error (AccessDenied) occurred when calling the
GetBucketLocation operation: Access Denied

$ aws s3api get-object --bucket ${bucket} \
--key ${object} output_file.txt \
--profile ${profile}
A client error (AccessDenied) occurred when calling the GetObject
operation: Access Denied
```

See also

- *Example 2: Bucket Owner Granting Cross-Account Bucket Permissions*
  http://docs.aws.amazon.com/AmazonS3/latest/dev/example-walkthroughs-managing-access-example2.html

- *Walkthrough: Delegating Access Across AWS Accounts Using IAM Roles*
  http://docs.aws.amazon.com/IAM/latest/UserGuide/roles-walkthrough-crossacct.html

Walkthrough 3: To grant cross-account bucket permissions to objects without ownership

Walkthrough 1 is almost similar to walkthrough 2. The difference is that the bucket owner in Account A wants to grant permissions of its bucket to their user. However, the owner does not own all objects in the bucket and wants to allows its users to access to objects it does not own, but are instead, owned by a user in Account B. The following diagram shows how AWS Account A grants permissions to the S3 bucket, and the Admin IAM user in AWS Account A delegates permissions to a different IAM user in its account to access the objects owned by the IAM user in Account B for this walkthrough.

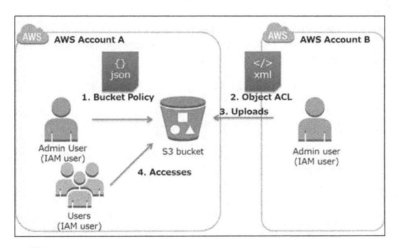

To summarize, what you need to do is:

1. Create a bucket policy in Account A with two statements—one to grant cross-account permission to Account B to upload objects, and the other to allow users in Account A to access the objects in the bucket.

2. Upload objects to the bucket owned by Account A in Account B.

3. Update objects ACL with permissions to give the bucket owner full control on the objects.

4. Verify that the IAM users in Account A are granted permission to access the objects in the bucket.

We refer to the AWS account ID, the AWS account, and the administrator user as follows:

AWS Account ID	Account Referred to as	Administrator user in the account
1111-1111-1111	Account A	AccountAadmin
2222-2222-2222	Account B	AccountBadmin

Getting ready

All you need to do is to follow almost the same steps as shown in walkthrough 1.

How to do it...

First, we create a bucket and attach a bucket policy to the bucket in Account A to grant cross-account permissions to Account B, and then check whether Account B can perform the operations using AccountBadmin credentials.

Next, we create an IAM user called John and delegate permissions to the IAM user in Account B.

Lastly, check whether the permissions work using the credentials from John by uploading a sample object into the bucket owned by Account A with AWS CLI.

The first step is to create a bucket and an IAM user, attach a bucket policy in Account A, and verify that AccountBadmin can upload objects:

1. Sign in to the AWS management console using the AccountAadmin credentials and move to the S3 console at `https://console.aws.amazon.com/s3/`.

2. Create a bucket following the instruction, *How to configure a static website on Amazon S3 bucket* from Chapter 2, *Hosting a Static Website on Amazon S3 Bucket*.

3. In the IAM console, create an IAM user, John, to operate the S3 bucket following the instructions at *Walkthrough 1: To grant users bucket permissions* and note down the credentials.

4. Attach the bucket policy below on the bucket you created following the instruction at *Walkthrough 1 To grant users bucket permissions*:

   ❑ `AccountA-ID` is to be replaced with AWS Account A ID

   ❑ `AccountB-ID` is to be replaced with AWS Account B ID

   ❑ `S3BucketName` is to be replaced with the bucket name

   ❑ `IAMUserName` is to be replaced with the IAM user name:

   ```
   {
      "Version": "2012-10-17",
      "Statement": [
   ```

```
              {
                "Sid": "AccountBPermissions",
                "Effect": "Allow",
                "Principal": {
                  "AWS": "arn:aws:iam::AccountB-ID:root"
                },
                "Action": [
                  "s3:PutObject*",
                  "s3:GetObject*"
                ],
                "Resource": "arn:S3BucketName/*"
              },
              {
                "Sid": "AccountAPermissions",
                "Effect": "Allow",
                "Principal": {
                  "AWS": "arn:aws:iam::AccountA-ID:user/IAMUserName"
                },
                "Action": "s3:GetObject",
                "Resource": "arn:S3BucketName/*"
              }
          ]
      }
```

5. Update the AWS config file of Account B credentials by entering its IAM credentials:

```
$ vim ~/.aws/config
[profile AccountBadmin]
aws_access_key_id = access-key
aws_secret_access_key = secret-access-key
region = us-east-1
```

6. Check whether AccountBadmin can upload objects to the bucket owned by Account A with the AccountBadmin credentials:

```
$ bucket=your-bucket-name
$ object=test.txt
$ aws s3api put-object \
--bucket ${bucket} \
--key ${object} \
--body ${object} \
--profile AccountBadmin
```

The second step is to add object ACLs to the bucket using AccountBadmin credentials:

1. Sign in to the AWS management console using root credentials of Account A, navigate to **Security Credentials** at https://console.aws.amazon.com/iam/home#security_credential.

2. Click on **Account Identifiers** and you can see the **Canonical User ID** field shown in the following screenshot:

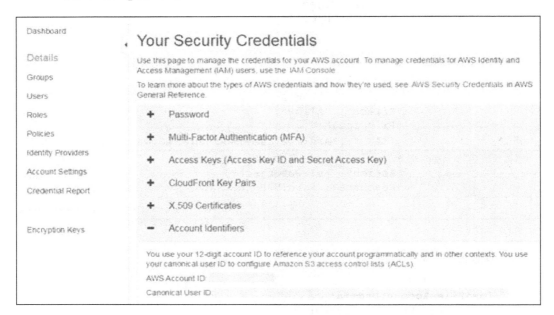

 You must use root account credentials to retrieve your canonical user ID. You cannot retrieve your canonical user ID using IAM user credentials.

3. Add a grant in the object ACL to the object to allow the bucket owner to have full control of the object with AccountBadmin credentials:

```
$ canonical_id=AccountA-CanonicalID
$ profile=AccountBadmin
$ aws s3api put-object-acl \
--bucket ${bucket} \
--key ${object} \
--grant-full-control id=${canonical_id} \
--profile ${profile}
```

4. Check whether the ACL of the object is associated with `AccountA-CanonicalID` in the `Grants` section shown in the following result:

```
$ aws s3api get-object-acl \
--bucket ${bucket} \
--key ${object} \
--profile ${profile}
{
    "Owner": {
        "DisplayName": "AccountB",
        "ID": "${AccountB-CanonicalID}"
    },
    "Grants": [
        {
            "Grantee": {
                "DisplayName": "AccountA",
                "ID": "${AccountA-CanonicalID}"
            },
            "Permission": "FULL_CONTROL"
        }
    ]
}
```

If you put objects without adding object ACLs, the ACL of the object is associated with `AccountB-CanonicalID` in the following result:

```
$ aws s3api get-object-acl \
--bucket ${bucket} \
--key ${object} \
--profile ${profile}
{
    "Owner": {
        "DisplayName": "AccountB",
        "ID": "${AccountB-CanonicalID}"
    },
    "Grants": [
        {
            "Grantee": {
                "DisplayName": "AccountB",
                "ID": "${AccountB-CanonicalID}"
            },
            "Permission": "FULL_CONTROL"
        }
    ]
}
```

How it works...

As we finished configuring the bucket policy on the bucket, creating the IAM user in Account A, uploading an object to the bucket, and adding an object ACL to the object in Account B, let's see how they work using AWS CLI to verify the permissions.

First, we update the AWS CLI config file for John, and then verify that the object created by AccountBadmin can be retrieved using the credentials from John:

1. Update the AWS config file of John's credentials by entering its IAM credentials:

    ```
    $ vim ~/.aws/config
    [profile UserJohn]
    aws_access_key_id = access-key
    aws_secret_access_key = secret-access-key
    region = us-east-1
    ```

2. Check whether `UserJohn` can list the bucket:

    ```
    $ bucket=your-bucket-name
    $ profie=UserJohn
    $ aws s3api get-object \
    --bucket ${bucket} \
    --key ${object} object_output.txt
    --profile ${profile}
    ```

Let's examine each element in the bucket policy and the user policy so that we can understand how the bucket policy and the user policy work to grant cross-account bucket permissions to objects without ownership.

The bucket policy

The difference between walkthroughs 1, 2, and 3 is that the bucket policy uses the `Sid` element and there are two statements in the policy. Let's look into the preceding policy and examine each component.

In the first `Sid` element called `AccountBPermissions`, the policy allows AccountB ID to perform the `s3::GetObject` and `s3::PutObject` actions in a specific bucket to put objects and add object ACLs to objects:

```
"Sid": "AccountBPermissions",
"Effect": "Allow",
"Principal": {
  "AWS": "arn:aws:iam::AccountB-ID:root"
},
"Action": [
```

```
    "s3:PutObject*",
    "s3:GetObject*"
  ],
  "Resource": "arn:S3BucketName/*"
```

In the second `Sid` element called `AccountAPermissions`, the policy allows `IAMUserName` in AccountA-ID to perform the `s3::GetObject` actions in a specific bucket to get objects in the bucket, so that `UserJohn` can get the objects owned by AccountBadmin, even if John does not have the ownership of the object:

```
  "Sid": "AccountAPermissions",
  "Effect": "Allow",
  "Principal": {
    "AWS": "arn:aws:iam::AccountA-ID:user/IAMUserName"
  },
  "Action": "s3:GetObject",
  "Resource": "arn:S3BucketName/*"
}
```

See also

▶ *Example 3: Bucket Owner Granting Its Users Permissions to Objects It Does Not Own* at `http://docs.aws.amazon.com/AmazonS3/latest/dev/example-walkthroughs-managing-access-example3.html`

Walkthrough 4: Bucket and user policy examples

This section introduces more practical examples to configure complex policies specifying actions, buckets, or conditions based on several realistic scenarios.

Getting ready

Through the walkthroughs, you learned about the concept of bucket policies and user policies, how to configure bucket policies to Amazon S3 bucket and user policies to IAM users, and how bucket policies and user policies work together.

This section focuses on bucket policy examples and their structure based on common use cases. We will be looking into the following bucket policy examples:

▶ Granting permissions to multiple accounts, specific resources, and addresses in a bucket policy

▶ Allowing a user to access a folder in a bucket in a specific region in a user policy

How to do it...

The first scenario is where we want to allow a specific user in the AWS accounts to access two buckets configuring a bucket policy, the actions only Put and Get for the bucket and only from specific networks to restrict access to the bucket.

Granting permissions to multiple accounts, specific resources, and addresses in a bucket policy

To summarize the conditions, the bucket policy meets the following requirements:

Principal	username-a in AccountA
(AWS Account and User)	username-b in AccountB
Action	GetObject
	PutObject
Resource	bucket-a
(Bucket)	bucket-b
Condition	10.1.1.0/24 (except for 10.1.1.0/30)
(Source IP address)	10.10.1.0/24 (except for 10.10.1.0/30)

First, we create a bucket and attach a bucket policy to the bucket in Account A, and then create an IAM user called `username-a` in Account A and `username-b` in Account B. Lastly, attach a bucket policy to the bucket owned by Account A.

1. Sign in to the AWS management console in Account A and move to the S3 console at `https://console.aws.amazon.com/s3/`.

2. Create a bucket in Account A and in Account B following the instructions, *How to configure a static website on Amazon S3 bucket* from *Chapter 2, Hosting a Static Website on Amazon S3 Bucket*.

3. In the IAM console, create an IAM user, `username-a` in Account A and an IAM user, `username-b` in Account B following the instructions at *Walkthrough 1: To grant users bucket permissions*.

4. Attach the bucket policy on the bucket you created by following the instructions at *Walkthrough 1: To grant users bucket permissions*:

   ❑ `AcountA-ID` is to be replaced with AWS Account A ID

   ❑ `AccountB-ID` is to be replaced with AWS Account B ID:

   ```
   {
       "Version": "2012-10-17",
       "Statement": [
         {
   ```

```
              "Sid": "AddCannedAcl",
              "Effect": "Allow",
              "Principal": {
                "AWS": [
                  "arn:aws:iam::AccountA-ID:user/username-a",
                  "arn:aws:iam::AccountB-ID:user/username-b"
                ]
              },
              "Action": [
                "s3:GetObject",
                "s3:PutObject"
              ],
              "Resource": [
                "arn:aws:s3:::bucket-a/*",
                "arn:aws:s3:::bucket-b/*"
              ],
              "Condition": {
                "IpAddress": {
                  "aws:SourceIp": [
                    "10.1.1.0/24",
                    "10.10.1.0/24"
                  ]
                },
                "NotIpAddress": {
                  "aws:SourceIp": [
                    "10.1.1.0/30",
                    "10.10.1.0/30"
                  ]
                }
              }
          }
        ]
      }
```

Allowing a user to access a folder in a bucket in a specific region in a user policy

The second scenario is where we will allow an IAM group to perform operations such as putting, getting, and deleting objects in a folder in a specific bucket configuring a user policy and attaching the policy to the IAM group. In addition, we want to grant permissions to the folders in the bucket by the requester's username instead of attaching policies to individual users. For example, if username-a sends a request to put an object, the operation is allowed only if username-a is uploading the object to the `bucket-a/username-a` folder.

To summarize the conditions, the policy meets the following requirements:

IAM user	username-a
	username-b
Action	GetObject
	PutObject
	DeleteteObject
Resource (Bucket)	bucket-a/{requester's user name}/*

First, we create a bucket and then two IAM users, username-a and username-b. Next, we create a user policy, an IAM group, and attach the policy to the IAM group. Finally, we verify and check whether the permissions of the policy work as we intended.

1. Sign in to the AWS management console in Account A and move to the S3 console at `https://console.aws.amazon.com/s3/`.

2. Create a bucket following the instructions in *How to configure a static website on Amazon S3 bucket* from *Chapter 2, Hosting a Static Website on Amazon S3 Bucket*.

3. Sign in to the AWS management console and redirect it to the IAM console at `https://console.aws.amazon.com/iam/`.

4. Create an IAM user username-a and username-b following the instructions in *The first step....*

5. In the **Dashboard** section, on the left-hand side, click on **Policies** and **Create Policy**:

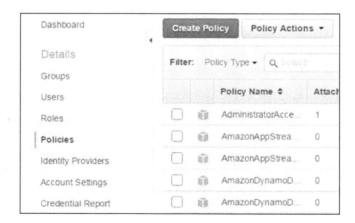

6. In the **Create Your Own Policy** section, click on **Select**:

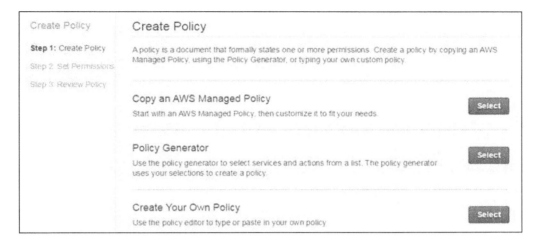

7. Attach the following policy and click on **Create Policy,** as shown in the following screenshot:

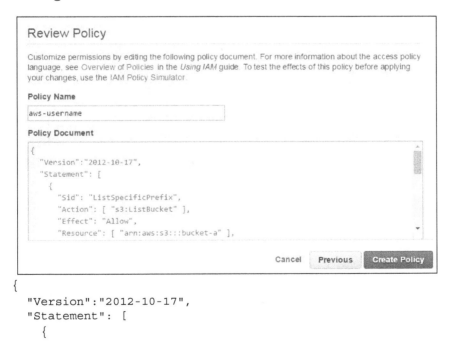

```
{
    "Version":"2012-10-17",
    "Statement": [
        {
```

```
        "Sid": "ListSpecificPrefix",
        "Action": [ "s3:ListBucket" ],
        "Effect": "Allow",
        "Resource": [ "arn:aws:s3:::bucket-a" ],
        "Condition": {
          "StringLike": {
            "s3:prefix": [ "${aws:username}/*" ]
            }
          }
      },
      {
        "Sid": "AllowOperations",
        "Effect":"Allow",
        "Action":[
          "s3:PutObject",
          "s3:GetObject",
          "s3:DeleteObject"
        ],
        "Resource":"arn:aws:s3:::bucket-a/${aws:username}/*"
      }
    ]
  }
```

8. In the **Dashboard** section on the left-hand side, click on **Groups** and **Create New Group**:

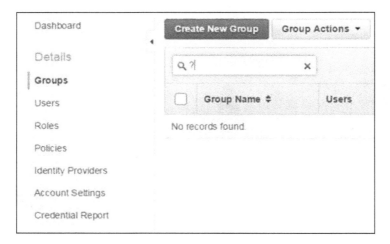

9. In the **Group Name** box, enter a group name, and click on **Next Step**:

10. In the **Policy Type** box, enter the policy name, choose the policy, and then click on **Next Step**:

11. After reviewing the configuration, click on **Create Group**:

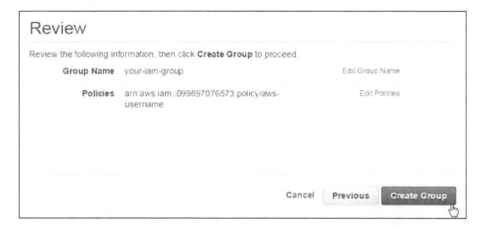

How it works...

Let's look into the preceding scenarios and examine each component.

Granting permissions to multiple accounts, specific resources and addresses in a bucket policy

In the `Principal` element, userA in AccountA and userB in AccountB are identified and allowed to access. `arn:aws:iam::AccountA-ID:user/username-a` defines that it grants permissions to username-a in the AWS account:

```
"Principal": {
  "AWS": [
    "arn:aws:iam::AccountA-ID:user/username-a",
    "arn:aws:iam::AccountB-ID:user/username-b"
  ]
```

In the `Action` element, the `s3::GetObject` and `s3::PutObject` actions are defined and allowed:

```
"Action": [
  "s3:GetObject",
  "s3:PutObject"
],
```

In the `Resource` element, `arn:aws:s3:::bucket-a/*` defines that any object under `bucket-a` is allowed to access:

```
"Resource": [
  "arn:aws:s3:::bucket-a/*",
  "arn:aws:s3:::bucket-b/*"
],
```

In the `Condition` element, `Ipaddress` and `NotIpaddress` are a key-value pair and the condition. The key-pair uses the `aws:SourceIp` key and CIDR as values. The reason why both `Ipaddress` and `NotIpaddress` are used is because it allows `10.1.1.0/24` but for `10.1.1.0/30` specifying the two conditions:

```
"Condition": {
  "IpAddress": {
    "aws:SourceIp": [
      "10.1.1.0/24",
      "10.10.1.0/24"
    ]
  },
  "NotIpAddress": {
    "aws:SourceIp": [
      "10.1.1.0/30",
      "10.10.1.0/30"
    ]
  }
}
```

Allowing a user to access a folder in a bucket in a specific region in a user policy

As we created a bucket, IAM users, and an IAM group, and configured the user policy to the IAM group, let's look into the policy and examine each component.

In the first `Sid` element called `ListSpecificPrefix`, the policy `${aws:username}` variable is replaced by the requester's username and allows a set of permissions to list buckets in the `bucket-a/${aws:username}` folder:

```
"Sid": "ListSpecificPrefix",
"Action": [ "s3:ListBucket" ],
"Effect": "Allow",
"Resource": [ "arn:aws:s3:::bucket-a" ],
"Condition": {
  "StringLike": {
    "s3:prefix": [ "${aws:username}/*" ]
  }
}
```

In the second `Sid` element called `AllowOperations`, the policy `${aws:username}` variable is replaced by the requester's username and allows a set of permissions to put, get, and delete objects in the `bucket-a/${aws:username}` folder:

```
"Sid": "AllowOperations",
"Effect":"Allow",
"Action":[
  "s3:PutObject",
  "s3:GetObject",
  "s3:DeleteObject"
],
"Resource":"arn:aws:s3:::bucket-a/${aws:username}/*"
```

To verify the policy, we create two IAM users called username-a and username-b, attach the IAM group policy to the users, and then verify the permissions to the folders by the requester's username using each user's credentials.

First, username-a can get, put, and delete objects in the `username-a` folder in the bucket, as shown in the following result:

```
$ bucket=bucket-a
$ user_a=username-a
$ user_b=username-b
$ object=test.txt

$ aws s3 ls s3://${bucket}/${user_a}/ --profile ${user_a}
                        PRE username-a/

$ aws s3 cp ${object} s3://${bucket}/${user_a}/ --profile ${user_a}
upload: ./test.txt to s3://bucket-a/username-a/test.txt

$ aws s3 rm s3://${bucket}/${user_a}/${object} --profile ${user_a}
delete: s3://bucket-a/username-a/test.txt
```

Second, username-a cannot get, put, and delete objects in the `username-b` folder in the bucket, as shown in the following result:

```
$ aws s3 ls s3://${bucket}/${user_b}/ --profile ${user_a}
A client error (AccessDenied) occurred when calling the ListObjects
operation: Access Denied

$ aws s3 cp ${object} s3://${bucket}/${user_b}/ --profile ${user_a}
upload failed: ./test.txt to s3://bucket-for-policy03//test.txt A
client error (AccessDenied) occurred when calling the PutObject
operation: Access Denied
```

Let's do it again and replace username-a with username-b.

First, username-b can get, put, and delete objects in the `username-b` folder in the bucket, as shown in the following result:

```
$ aws s3 ls s3://${bucket}/${user_b}/ --profile ${user_b}
2015-02-21 16:45:53            0

$ aws s3 cp ${object} s3://${bucket}/${user_b}/ --profile ${user_b}
upload: ./test.txt to s3://bucket-for-policy03/username-b/test.txt

$ aws s3 rm s3://${bucket}/${user_b}/${object} --profile ${user_b}
delete: s3://bucket-for-policy03/username-b/test.txt
```

Second, username-b cannot get, put, and delete objects in the `username-a` folder in the bucket, as shown in the following result:

```
$ aws s3 ls s3://${bucket}/${user_a}/ --profile ${user_b}
A client error (AccessDenied) occurred when calling the ListObjects
operation: Access Denied

$ aws s3 cp ${object} s3://${bucket}/${user_a}/ --profile ${user_b}
upload failed: ./test.txt to s3://bucket-for-policy03/username-
a/test.txt A client error (AccessDenied) occurred when calling the
PutObject operation: Access Denied
```

The `${aws:username}` variable is friendly to identify their user names, but they are required to be globally unique. The problem is that if user Tom leaves the organization and another Tom joins the organization, the new Tom could have access to the old Tom's resources. Instead of using usernames, you can use the `${aws:userid}` variable to create folders based on each user's IDs.

For more information, see `http://docs.aws.amazon.com/IAM/latest/UserGuide/PolicyVariables.html`.

7

Sending Authenticated Requests with AWS SDKs

In this chapter, you will learn:

- ▶ How to make requests using IAM user temporary credentials with AWS SDK
- ▶ How to make requests using federated user temporary credentials with AWS SDK

Introduction

In *Chapter 6, Securing Resources with Bucket Policies and IAM,* you not only learned how to secure your buckets or objects using bucket policies and user policies but also how to manage common operations for an S3 bucket with AWS SDKs, which we came across in *Chapter 1, Managing Common Operations with AWS SDKs.* In the real world, for example, when you make your applications, you will need to use methods in the library or SDK to simplify using AWS services in your application. We will follow how to use AWS SDKs to make requests using the IAM user's temporary credentials with AWS SDKs.

How to make requests using IAM user temporary credentials with AWS SDK

There are situations where you need to grant permissions to temporarily access Amazon S3 resources. For example, your applications create temporary users to get objects in an S3 bucket for a certain period of time and the permissions granted to the temporary user need to be disabled or removed after the duration expires. IAM users support to request temporary security credentials using the **AWS Security Token Service** (**AWS STS**).You will learn how to make requests using IAM user temporary credentials with AWS SDK for PHP.

For further information about the AWS Security Token Service (AWS STS), see http://docs.aws.amazon.com/STS/latest/UsingSTS/Welcome.html.

Getting ready

As we use AWS SDK for PHP in this chapter, you need to have the AWS SDK for PHP properly installed in your server or client PC. Install AWS SDK for PHP following the instruction *Learning AWS SDK for PHP and basic S3 operations with sample code* from *Chapter 1, Managing Common Operations with AWS SDKs*.

How to do it...

First, we create an IAM policy to allow temporary security credentials for IAM users and list the bucket action, and then attach the policy to an IAM group. Next, we create an IAM user to make requests using temporary security credentials. Finally, we use the IAM user's temporary security credentials and list objects in a bucket using a sample PHP script:

1. Sign in to the AWS management console and move to the S3 console at https://console.aws.amazon.com/s3/.

2. Create a bucket following the instructions in *How to configure a static website on Amazon S3 bucket* from *Chapter 2, Hosting a Static Website on Amazon S3 Bucket*.

3. Create an IAM policy and IAM group, and attach the policy to the IAM group, then create an IAM user and note down the credentials following the instructions at *Walkthrough 1-4Bucket and User policy examples: Allowing a user to access to a folder in a bucket in a specific region in a user policy*. The policy to be attached to your IAM group is as follows:

S3BucketName is to be replaced with the Bucket name.

```
{
  "Version": "2012-10-17",
  "Statement": [
    {
      "Effect": "Allow",
      "Action": [
        "sts:GetFederationToken*",
        "s3:ListBucket"
      ],
      "Resource": [
        "*"
      ]
    },
    {
      "Effect": "Allow",
      "Action": [
        "s3:ListBucket"
      ],
      "Resource": [
        "arn:aws:s3:::S3BucketName"
      ]
    }
  ]
}
```

4. Update the AWS config file by entering the IAM credentials:

```
$ aws configure
AWS Access Key ID [None]: access-key
AWS Secret Access Key [None]: secret-access-key
Default region name [None]: us-east-1
Default output format [None]:
```

How it works...

As we have configured an IAM policy to allow IAM users to use temporary security credentials and an IAM group, attached the IAM policy to the IAM group, create an IAM user, and attach the IAM user to the IAM group. Here, we will be making S3 requests using temporary security credentials and a sample PHP script.

1. Download the sample SDK application:

```
$ git clone https://github.com/awslabs/aws-php-sample.git
$ cd aws-php-sample/
```

2. Set up the following sample PHP script under the `aws-php-sample` directory:

```php
<?php

// Include the AWS SDK using the Composer autoloader.
require 'vendor/autoload.php';

// Retrieve variable from command-line
$bucket = $argv[1];
$duration = $argv[2];

use Aws\Sts\StsClient;
use Aws\S3\S3Client;
use Aws\S3\Exception\S3Exception;

$sts = StsClient::factory();

$credentials = $sts->getSessionToken()->get('Credentials');
$s3 = S3Client::factory(array(
    'key'    => $credentials['AccessKeyId'],
    'secret' => $credentials['SecretAccessKey'],
    'token'  => $credentials['SessionToken'],
    'DurationSeconds'  => $duration
));

// debugging credentials
echo "## -- AWS IAM Credentials for debugging -- ##" .
"\n";
echo "AccessKeyId: " . $credentials['AccessKeyId']  . "\n";
echo "SecretAccessKey: " . $credentials['SecretAccessKey']
. "\n";
echo "SessionToken: " . $credentials['SessionToken']  .
"\n";
echo "\n";

try {
    $objects = $s3->getIterator('ListObjects', array(
        'Bucket' => $bucket
    ));

echo "## -- Objects in bucket: $bucket -- ##" . "\n";
echo "LastModified" . "\t\t\t" . "Size" . "\t\t" . "Object"
. "\n";
```

```
foreach ($objects as $object) {
echo $object['LastModified'] . "\t" . $object['Size'] .
"\t" . $object['Key'] . "\n";
    }
    echo "\n";
} catch (S3Exception $e) {
echo $e->getMessage() . "\n";
}
```

3. Set the S3 bucket name referred to as `bucket`, and the session duration referred to as `duration`, and then execute the sample PHP script using the following command:

```
$ bucket=S3BucketName
$ duration=session-duration
$ phpsample_code.php $bucket $duration
## -- AWS IAM Credentials for debugging -- ##
AccessKeyId: access-key
SecretAccessKey: secret-access-key
SessionToken: session-token

## -- Objects in bucket: hashnao-policy-test -- ##
LastModified                    Size        Object
2015-03-02T00:33:41.000Z        1048576 file_001.txt
2015-03-02T00:33:43.000Z        2097152 file_002.txt
2015-03-02T00:33:47.000Z        3145728 file_003.txt
```

 You can specify the duration in seconds between 1 and 36 hours. The session duration is 1 hour (which is 3,600 seconds), by default.

Finally, let's examine the sample PHP script so that we can understand which method requests temporary security credentials, and requests to access the objects in the bucket using the temporary security credentials.

The following class methods import functions as follows:

▶ The `Aws\Sts\StsClient` class creates a new Amazon STS client object

▶ The `Aws\S3\S3Client` class creates a new Amazon S3 client

▶ The `Aws\S3\Exception/S3Exception` class imports a default service exception class:

```
use Aws\Sts\StsClient;
use Aws\S3\S3Client;
use Aws\S3\Exception\S3Exception;
```

The `getSessionToken` call returns a set of temporary credentials for an IAM user and the credentials consist of an access key ID, a secret access key, and a security token in the array:

```
$credentials = $sts->getSessionToken()->get('Credentials');
$s3 = S3Client::factory(array(
    'key'    => $credentials['AccessKeyId'],
    'secret' => $credentials['SecretAccessKey'],
    'token'  => $credentials['SessionToken'],
'DurationSeconds'  => $duration
));
```

In the following part, the `getIterator` method calls operations and enumerates through the resources from a result set with `foreach`, iterates objects in the bucket, and then displays the `LastModified` property, the `size` property, and the `key` property. Finally, it catches the exception in the `S3Exception` class and displays its messages:

```
try {
    $objects = $s3->getIterator('ListObjects', array(
        'Bucket' => $bucket
    ));
echo "## -- Objects in bucket: $bucket -- ##" . "\n";
echo "LastModified" . "\t\t\t" . "Size" . "\t\t" . "Object" . "\n";
foreach ($objects as $object) {
echo $object['LastModified'] . "\t" . $object['Size'] . "\t" .
$object['Key'] . "\n";
    }
echo "\n";
} catch (S3Exception $e) {
echo $e->getMessage() . "\n";
}
```

See also

> ▸ *Making Requests Using AWS Account or IAM User Temporary Credentials - AWS SDK for PHP* at http://docs.aws.amazon.com/AmazonS3/latest/dev/AuthUsingTempSessionTokenPHP.html

> ▸ *Granting Permissions to Create Temporary Security Credentials* at http://docs.aws.amazon.com/STS/latest/UsingSTS/STSPermission.html

How to make requests using federated user temporary credentials with AWS SDK

We configured IAM users to control permissions of each IAM user to access AWS resources. AWS IAM supports identify federation as external identities, to securely access to your AWS resources without the necessity of creating IAM users. We can provide permissions to the federated user using temporary credentials without having to create IAM users.

> For further information about Federation Management, see http://aws.amazon.com/iam/details/manage-federation/.

Getting ready

As we use AWS SDK for PHP in this chapter, you need to have the AWS SDK for PHP properly installed in your server or client PC. Install AWS SDK for PHP following the instructions in the *Learning AWS SDK for PHP and basic S3 operations with sample code* section of *Chapter 1, Managing Common Operations with AWS SDKs*.

How to do it...

First, we create an IAM policy to allow temporary security credentials for federated users and list bucket actions, and then attach the policy to an IAM group. Next, we create an IAM user to make requests using temporary security credentials. Finally, we grant permissions for a federated user and list objects in a bucket using a sample PHP script:

1. Sign in to the AWS management console and move to the S3 console at https://console.aws.amazon.com/s3/.

2. Create a bucket following the instructions in the *How to configure a static website on Amazon S3 bucket* section of *Chapter 2, Hosting a Static Website on Amazon S3 Bucket*.

3. Create an IAM policy, IAM group, and attach the policy to the IAM group, then create an IAM user and note down the credentials following the instructions at *Walkthrough 1-4Bucket and User policy examples: Allowing a user to access to a folder in a bucket in a specific region in a user policy*. The policy to be attached to your IAM group is as follows:

    S3BucketName is to be replaced with the Bucket name.

    ```
    {
        "Version": "2012-10-17",
    ```

```
  "Statement": [
    {
      "Effect": "Allow",
      "Action": [
        "sts:GetSessionToken*",
        "s3:ListBucket"
      ],
      "Resource": [
        "*"
      ]
    },
    {
      "Effect": "Allow",
      "Action": [
        "s3:ListBucket"
      ],
      "Resource": [
        "arn:aws:s3:::S3BucketName"
      ]
    }
  ]
}
```

4. Update the AWS config file entering the IAM credentials:

```
$ aws configure
AWS Access Key ID [None]: access-key
AWS Secret Access Key [None]: secret-access-key
Default region name [None]: us-east-1
Default output format [None]:
```

How it works...

We have configured an IAM policy and an IAM group, attached the IAM policy to the IAM group, created an IAM user, and attached the IAM user to the IAM group. This is the final part to verify the permissions granted to the federated user:

1. Download the sample SDK application:

```
$ git clone https://github.com/awslabs/aws-php-sample.git
$ cdaws-php-sample/
```

2. Set the following sample PHP script under the `aws-php-sample` directory:

```php
<?php

// Include the AWS SDK using the Composer autoloader.
```

```php
require 'vendor/autoload.php';

// Retrive variable from command-line
$bucket = $argv[1];
$duration = $argv[2];

use Aws\Sts\StsClient;
use Aws\S3\S3Client;
use Aws\S3\Exception\S3Exception;

$sts = StsClient::factory();

$credentials = $sts->getSessionToken()->get('Credentials');
$s3 = S3Client::factory(array(
    'key'    => $credentials['AccessKeyId'],
    'secret' => $credentials['SecretAccessKey'],
    'token'  => $credentials['SessionToken'],
    'DurationSeconds'  => $duration

));

// debugging credentials
echo "## -- AWS IAM Credentials for debugging -- ##" .
"\n";
echo "AccessKeyId: " . $credentials['AccessKeyId'] . "\n";
echo "SecretAccessKey: " . $credentials['SecretAccessKey']
. "\n";
echo "SessionToken: " . $credentials['SessionToken'] .
"\n";
echo "\n";

try {
    $objects = $s3->getIterator('ListObjects', array(
        'Bucket' => $bucket
    ));

echo "## -- Objects in bucket: $bucket -- ##" . "\n";
echo "LastModified" . "\t\t\t" . "Size" . "\t\t" . "Object"
. "\n";
foreach ($objects as $object) {
echo $object['LastModified'] . "\t" . $object['Size'] .
"\t" . $object['Key'] . "\n";
    }
```

```
        echo "\n";
    } catch (S3Exception $e) {
    echo $e->getMessage() . "\n";
    }
```

3. Set the S3 bucket name referred to as `bucket`, and the federated username referred to as `user`, and the session duration referred to as `duration`, and then execute the sample PHP script using the following command:

```
$ bucket=S3BucketName
$ user=FederatedUserName
$ duration=session-duration
$ phpsample_code.php $bucket $duration
## -- AWS IAM Credentials for debugging -- ##
AccessKeyId: access-key
SecretAccessKey: secret-access-key
SessionToken: session-token

## -- Objects in bucket: hashnao-policy-test -- ##
LastModified                    Size         Object
2015-03-02T00:33:41.000Z        1048576 file_001.txt
2015-03-02T00:33:43.000Z        2097152 file_002.txt
2015-03-02T00:33:47.000Z        3145728 file_003.txt
```

 You can specify the duration in seconds between 1 and 36 hours. The session duration is 1 hour (which is 3,600 seconds), by default.

Finally, let's examine the sample PHP script so that we can understand which method makes requests to federated users and your applications and how federated users and your applications can send authenticated requests to access the objects in the bucket.

In the `StsClient::factory` method, several parameters, with key and value, are provided in its array and fetched the federated credentials as follows:

- `Name` is referred as the name of the federated user and used as an identifier for the temporary security credentials.

- `DurationSeconds` is the duration in seconds in which the session should last. The acceptable duration range is from 900 seconds (15 minutes) to 129,600 seconds (36 hours) and 43,200 seconds (12 hours), as the default.

▶ `Policy` defines an IAM policy in the JSON format and is passed with the GetFederationTokencall, and then evaluated along with the policy attached to the IAM user. The policy is used to define the permissions that are available to the IMA user:

```
$sts = StsClient::factory();
$credentials = $sts->getSessionToken()->get('Credentials');
$s3 = S3Client::factory(array(
    'key'    => $credentials['AccessKeyId'],
    'secret' => $credentials['SecretAccessKey'],
    'token'  => $credentials['SessionToken'],
    'DurationSeconds'  => $duration
));
```

The following part provides temporary security credentials in order to send authenticated requests to Amazon S3:

```
$credentials = $result->get('Credentials');
$s3 = S3Client::factory(array(
  'key'    => $credentials['AccessKeyId'],
  'secret' => $credentials['SecretAccessKey'],
  'token'  => $credentials['SessionToken']
));
```

See also

▶ *Making Requests Using AWS Account or IAM User Credentials – AWS SDK for PHP* at http://docs.aws.amazon.com/AmazonS3/latest/dev/AuthUsingAcctOrUserCredPHP.html

▶ *Permissions for GetFederationToken* at http://docs.aws.amazon.com/STS/latest/UsingSTS/permissions-get-federation-token.html

▶ AWS SDK for PHP in *Class StsClient* at http://docs.aws.amazon.com/aws-sdk-php/latest/class-Aws.Sts.StsClient.html

8

Protecting Data Using Server-side and Client-side Encryption

In this chapter, you will learn:

- ▸ How to protect data using server-side encryption
- ▸ How to protect data using client-side encryption

Introduction

When you need to securely upload or download your objects to the Amazon S3 bucket, you can use the HTTPS protocol via the SSL encrypted endpoints. In addition, Amazon S3 can automatically encrypt your data before saving it on disks in its data centers in a region and decrypt your data when you download it using **server-side encryption** (**SSE**) or use client libraries to encrypt your data before sending it to Amazon S3 using client-side encryption.

There is no difference in how you access encrypted or unencrypted data between server-side and client-side encryption, but there are different options for the encryption key between them. The following figure shows the process of how to encrypt data using server-side and client encryption.

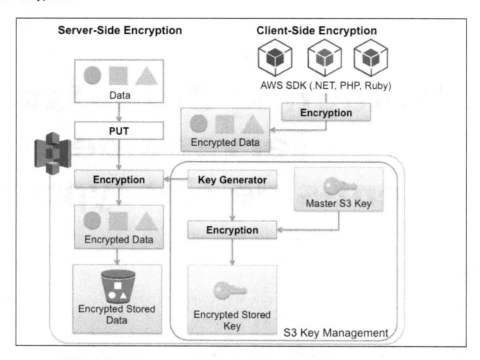

Server-side encryption provides three options to manage the encryption key:

 ▸   SSE with Amazon S3 key management (SSE-S3)

 ▸   SSE with AWS KMS (SSE-KMS)

 ▸   SSE with Customer-Provided keys (SSE-C)

Client-side encryption provides two options to manage encryption keys:

 ▸   AWS KMS-Managed Customer Master Key (CMK)

 ▸   Client-side Master Key

Depending on your situations, you can choose SSE or CSE to encrypt your data.

How to protect data using server-side encryption

When you are uploading objects or creating a copy of an existing object, you can encrypt your data by adding the `x-amz-server-side-encryption` header to the request.

You can specify server-side encryption using REST APIs and AWS SDKs that support wrapper API to request server-side encryption. In addition, you can use the AWS management console to upload objects and request server-side encryption.

Regarding server-side encryption, Amazon S3 encrypts your data at the object level with three options to manage the encryption keys:

> ▸ **SSE with Amazon S3 key management (SSE-S3)**: Server-side encryption with Amazon S3 manages encryption keys (SSE-S3) which use 256-bit Advanced Encryption Standard (AES-256) to encrypt your data and strong multifactor encryption to encrypt the key itself with a master key that is regularly rotated to enhance security.

> ▸ **SSE with AWS KMS (SSE-KMS)**: The difference between SSE-S3 and SSE-KMS is that SSE-KMS uses customer master keys (CMKs) to encrypt your objects and requires additional charges to use this service for additional benefits. You can create encryption keys, define the policies and audit keys usage using AWS KMS via the Encryption Keys section in the IAM console or AWS KMS APIs. The additional charge is for storing the AWS KMS key and for encrypting and decrypting requests to the objects.

> [For further information about SSE-KMS pricing, see the Amazon S3 example section, `https://aws.amazon.com/kms/pricing/`.]

> ▸ **SSE with Customer-Provided keys (SSE-C)**: The difference between SSE-S3, SSE-KMS, and SSE-C is in how the encryption keys are managed. SSE-C allows users to set your own encryption keys and Amazon S3 uses the encryption key and manages the encryption, writes data to the object, and decrypts them when accessing objects. As Amazon S3 does not store encryption keys, instead you need to track which encryption keys you provided for the encrypted objects.

The following table illustrates the availability of server-side encryption and AWS SDKs:

	SSE-S3	SSE-KMS	SSE-C
AWS SDK for Java	Available	Available	Available
AWS SDK for .NET	Available	Available	Available
AWS SDK for PHP	Available	-	-
AWS SDK for Ruby	Available	-	-
REST API	Available	-	Available
AWS Management Console	Available	-	-
AWS CLI	Available	Available	Available

Getting ready

You do not have to request or fill in any form to encrypt objects on Amazon S3 or pay any initial cost for SSE-S3, either. All you need to do is:

▶ Sign up on AWS and access the S3 console with your IAM credentials

▶ Install AWS CLI on your PC

How to do it...

We will now try out one of the three options, SSE with Amazon S3 key management (SSE-S3), to encrypt your data through the S3 console and AWS CLI.

First, let's try using the AWS management console to use SSE because you don't need anything but the permission to access the S3 console. All you need to do is simply enable server-side encryption specifying the object in the console. Follow these steps:

1. Sign in to the AWS management console and move to the S3 console at `https://console.aws.amazon.com/s3`.

2. In the S3 console, choose the bucket, and the object you want to encrypt as shown in the following screenshot:

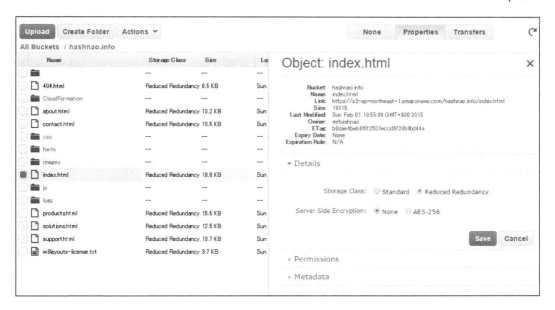

3. Pull down the **Details** section and in the **Server Side Encryption:** section, choose **AES-256** and click on **Save**.

The following instruction is to put your objects using server-side encryption with AWS CLI. It is simple to use server-side encryption with AWS CLI as well.

4. Put objects and specify the algorithm that will be used for encryption with the following command:

```
$ bucket=your-bucket-name
$ key=your-object
$ aws s3api put-object \
--bucket $bucket \
--key $key \
--server-side-encryption AES256
{
    "ETag": "\"d41d8cd98f00b204e9800998ecf8427e\"",
    "ServerSideEncryption": "AES256"
}
```

How it works...

After you have finished encrypting the object, you can see that the `x-amz-server-side-encryption` header is added to the object and the object is encrypted in AES256 with the curl command simply checking its header. The following result shows that the object header has been encrypted with SSE-S3:

```
$ curl --head https://s3-ap-northeast-
1.amazonaws.com/hashnao.info/index.html
HTTP/1.1 200 OK
x-amz-id-2:
RBL6BkkDqExD/4EpuPsEjxO7mXGhdruJ8Od4zqIQ29scoU4mtvAuzEQIOIpAgnSPOy+of
4amY1A=
x-amz-request-id: 5AD8E5BA06EE0329
Date: Wed, 18 Mar 2015 00:11:32 GMT
Last-Modified: Tue, 17 Mar 2015 23:51:14 GMT
ETag: "b0dae4beb6f0f2501eccd6f23b0bd44a"
x-amz-server-side-encryption: AES256
Accept-Ranges: bytes
Content-Type: text/html
Content-Length: 19316
Server: AmazonS3
```

The following result shows the status of the object before it is encrypted. You can see that the x-amz-server-side-encryption header is not added to the object header:

```
$ curl --head https://s3-ap-northeast-1.amazonaws.com/hashnao.info/index.
html
HTTP/1.1 200 OK
```

```
x-amz-id-2: WXSVGPt0314VAVr6ExrUlW2uLF2HDWj7rkkiPD9HSJ5iTyy019GE6VaJMTg7C
Ywm+LmEvA3bIqU=
x-amz-request-id: 8534D77C7A783C09
Date: Wed, 18 Mar 2015 00:19:11 GMT
Last-Modified: Wed, 18 Mar 2015 00:19:03 GMT
ETag: "b0dae4beb6f0f2501eccd6f23b0bd44a"
Accept-Ranges: bytes
Content-Type: text/html
Content-Length: 19316
Server: AmazonS3
```

You can also see the object header using AWS CLI with the following command:

```
$ bucket=your-bucket-name
$ key=your-object
$ aws s3api head-object \
--bucket $bucket \
--key $key
```

The following result shows the status of the same bucket and the same object replaced with the AWS CLI (aws s3api) command:

```
$ bucket=hashnao.info
$ key=index.html
$ aws s3api head-object \
--bucket $bucket \
--key $key
{
    "AcceptRanges": "bytes",
    "ContentType": "text/html",
    "LastModified": "Tue, 17 Mar 2015 23:51:14 GMT",
    "ContentLength": "19316",
    "ETag": "\"b0dae4beb6f0f2501eccd6f23b0bd44a\"",
    "ServerSideEncryption": "AES256"
}
```

The following result shows the status of the object before it is encrypted with the AWS CLI (aws s3api) command. As we have already checked, the header before being encrypted with the curl command shows that the x-amz-server-side-encryption header is not added to the object header:

```
$ aws s3api head-object \
--bucket $bucket \
--key $key
{
    "LastModified": "Sun, 01 Feb 2015 01:55:04 GMT",
```

```
    "AcceptRanges": "bytes",
    "ETag": "\"b0dae4beb6f0f2501eccd6f23b0bd44a\"",
    "ContentType": "text/html",
    "ContentLength": "19316"
}
```

See also

▸ *Protecting Data Using Server-Side Encryption* at http://docs.aws.amazon.com/ AmazonS3/latest/dev/serv-side-encryption.html

▸ *Protecting Data Using Server-Side Encryption with Amazon S3-Managed Encryption Keys (SSE-S3)* at http://docs.aws.amazon.com/AmazonS3/latest/dev/ UsingServerSideEncryption.html

How to protect data using client-side encryption

To protect data using client-side encryption with AWS KMS-managed Customer Master Key (CMK) and client-side master key, you can specify client-side encryption using AWS SDKs. You can choose two options to manage the encryption keys:

When using client-side encryption, AWS SDKs use Amazon S3 encryption client to encrypt data and the data is encrypted before sending to the S3 bucket. Amazon S3 just receives encrypted data and does not encrypt or decrypt the data. Client-side encryption has two options for using encryption keys.

AWS KMS-managed customer master key (CMK)

When using the Amazon S3 encryption client in the AWS SDK, the client calls AWS KMS to verify that the user is allowed to use the customer master key. If so, KMS returns two versions of the data encryption key; a plaintext data key and a cipher blob of the data key encrypted with the customer master key. The encryption client later encrypts the data using the plaintext key and removes the key in the memory. The encrypted data key is sent to Amazon S3 and stored with the encrypted data in Amazon S3.

The client-side master key

The difference between AWS KMS-managed customer master key (CMK) and a client-side master key is that your client-side master key and your encrypted data are never sent to AWS. Amazon S3 encryption application generates a one-time use envelope symmetric key to encrypt the data of a single S3 object locally and encrypt the envelope key using the master key. The client uploads the envelope key as part of the metadata to identify the key used to encrypt the envelope key itself with the encrypted data, and then Amazon S3 saves the encrypted data key as object metadata (x-amz-meta-x-amz-key).

If you lose your encryption keys, you will never be able to decrypt your data because they are never sent to Amazon S3. You should securely store your key and your data, for example, storing the key in a file or using a separate key management system.

The following table illustrates the availability of AWS SDKs and client-side encryption:

	CMK	Clients	SSE-C
AWS SDK for Java	Available	Available	Available
AWS SDK for .NET	Available	Available	Available
AWS SDK for Ruby	Available	Available	Available

Getting ready

The requirement is the same as the server-side encryption. The difference is as follows:

▸ Note down the IAM credentials (Access key and secret access key)
▸ Install AWS CLI (1.3.25)
▸ Install Ruby (2.0)
▸ Install AWS SDK for Ruby (v1)

How to do it...

1. Update the AWS config file entering the IAM credentials:

```
$ aws configure
AWS Access Key ID [None]: your-access-key
AWS Secret Access Key [None]: your-secret-access-key
Default region name [None]: region
Default output format [None]:
```

2. Install AWS SDK for Ruby v1 with the following command:

```
$ gem install aws-sdk -v '~>1'
```

3. Store the following script in your environment.

4. Replace `region: 'region'` with the region that the S3 bucket belongs to. For example, if the S3 region belongs to Asia Pacific Tokyo, it should be as follows:

```
region: 'ap-northeast-1'

require 'aws-sdk-v1' # not 'aws-sdk'
require 'openssl'

AWS.config(
  region: 'region'
)
s3 = AWS::S3::Client.new
bucket = ARGV[0]
object = ARGV[1]
data = (0...8).map{ (65 + rand(26)).chr }.join

# Generate a string key
symmetric_key = OpenSSL::Cipher::AES256.new(:CBC).random_key
options = { :encryption_key => symmetric_key }
s3_object = AWS.s3.buckets[bucket].objects[object]

# Creating an encrypted object to S3
s3_object.write(data, options)

# Reading the object from S3 and decrypting
puts "# Reading the object from S3 and decrypting."
puts s3_object.read(options)

# Reading the object from S3 without decrypting
puts "# Reading the object from S3 without decrypting."
puts s3_object.read

# Deleting the encrypted object
s3_object.delete
```

How it works...

First of all, let's try the ruby script and see how the data is encrypted using client-side encryption. The script uses a symmetric key and creates an encrypted object in the bucket, and then reads the object and decrypts it with the symmetric key.

Set variables for your bucket and an object name, and execute the sample Ruby script as follows:

```
$ bucket=your-bucket-name
$ object=your-object
$ ruby s3_test.rb $bucket $object
# Reading the object from S3 and decrypting.
DIMBTQJG
# Reading the object from S3 without decrypting.
2$▨(▨▨E▨`a▨
```

The last one seems to have some garbled characters, but this is because the object is read without decrypting. Next, let's examine the script and see how it works one by one.

As AWS SDK for Ruby version 2 is released, it is necessary to specify the following statement to use version 1:

```
require 'aws-sdk-v1' # not 'aws-sdk'
```

The AWS.config class, the global configuration for AWS uses the configuration values defined in ~/.aws/credentials. The access key and the secret access key in the IAM credentials you specified are loaded:

```
AWS.config(
region: 'ap-northeast-1'
)
```

The following variables set the bucket name, the object name in the argument, and the data variable that generate random characters write in the object:

```
bucket = ARGV[0]
object = ARGV[1]
data = (0...8).map{ (65 + rand(26)).chr }.join
```

An AES key is used for symmetric encryption in the OpenSSL::Cipher::AES256.new class and it generates a new random one-time-use symmetric key. The key can be 128, 192, or 256 bit sizes:

```
symmetric_key = OpenSSL::Cipher::AES256.new(:CBC).random_key
options = { :encryption_key => symmetric_key }
```

Client-side encryption uses a process called envelope encryption. All encryption and decryption occurs within your application and your private encryption keys and your unencrypted data will never be sent to AWS.

The `s3_object.write(data, options)` object locally encrypts the object with the encrypted symmetric key and the `puts s3_object.read(options)` object reads the object in the bucket and decrypts it with the same key:

```
s3_object.write(data, options)
puts s3_object.read(options)
```

 For further information about AWS SDK for the Ruby (v1) class, see http://docs.aws.amazon.com/AWSRubySDK/latest/AWS/S3/S3Object.html.

The purpose of the `puts s3_object.read` object is to read the object without decryption to ensure the encryption:

```
puts s3_object.read
```

The following output shows the object header encrypted in client-side encryption. The encrypted envelope key is stored as the object metadata `x-amz-meta-x-amz-key` and an initialization vector (IV) is stored as the object metadata `x-amz-meta-x-amz-iv`:

```
$ curl --head https://s3-ap-northeast-1.amazonaws.com/hashnao.info/ruby.
txt
HTTP/1.1 200 OK
x-amz-id-2: F7sxleb9XeUwZBNDhrZnvCorA6oGNGiIwbenhUpw5Co9S05pwQ69JJTrwrb
78gXLWbt2bCFqWHs=
x-amz-request-id: D4AE0684074CDFED
Date: Thu, 19 Mar 2015 01:41:01 GMT
x-amz-meta-x-amz-iv: bYcCbFuuai6Vkq9QHKNwqA==
x-amz-meta-x-amz-unencrypted-content-length: 4
x-amz-meta-x-amz-matdesc: {}
x-amz-meta-x-amz-key:
GRehaSPqtEbNIP8iasgoVKRJMvuC5vE3wmhZDOQe6zOCn80FF2Qy6IRok5yE5NrQ
Last-Modified: Wed, 18 Mar 2015 09:22:52 GMT
ETag: "772bb14cf0f59decd3dccfdd172ffdd2"
Accept-Ranges: bytes
Content-Type:
Content-Length: 16
Server: AmazonS3
```

If you need to securely manage your maser key, you can choose to use a client-side master key method and the following AWS SDKs support client-side encryption:

- ► AWS SDK for Java
- ► AWS SDK for .NET
- ► AWS SDK for Ruby

See also

- *Protecting Data Using Client-Side Encryption* at `http://docs.aws.amazon.com/AmazonS3/latest/dev/UsingClientSideEncryption.html`

- *AWS SDK for Ruby - Version 1* at `http://docs.aws.amazon.com/AWSRubySDK/latest/`

- *Using Client-Side Encryption for S3 in the AWS SDK for Ruby* at `http://ruby.awsblog.com/post/Tx1OFBULXYZNVTH/Using-Client-Side-Encryption-for-S3-in-the-AWS-SDK-for-Ruby`

9

Enabling Cross-origin Resource Sharing

In this chapter, you will learn:

- ▶ Walkthrough 1: Enabling CORS through the S3 console
- ▶ Walkthrough 2: Enabling CORS using AWS CLI

Introduction

Cross-origin resource sharing (**CORS**) allows client web applications to access your S3 resources in a different domain by defining the CORS configuration in the XML document attached to your bucket. It allows cross-origin requests for your client-side application using CORS. For example, imagine that you have your own web server in the EC2 instance and want to use JavaScript on the web pages to access JSON files in an S3 static website. You can configure your bucket to enable cross-origin requests from the web server.

CORS can define rules in the XML configuration document, for example, the methods (GET, PUT, POST, DELETE, and HEAD), the origins (http://xxx, http://*.com), the headers (Authorization, Content-Type, x-amz-xxx, and so on), and the time in seconds to cache the response.

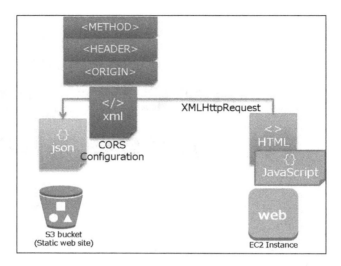

To enable CORS, the following methods are supported:

- ► The AWS management console
- ► AWS SDK for Java
- ► AWS SDK for JavaScript
- ► AWS SDK for .NET
- ► AWS SDK for PHP
- ► AWS SDK for Python
- ► AWS SDK for Ruby
- ► REST API
- ► AWS CLI

Walkthrough 1: Enabling CORS through the S3 console

This section introduces the process of enabling S3 CORS applying CORS configuration with your S3 buckets and checking if it works uploading a sample JSON code.

Getting ready

You do not have to request permissions to enable S3 CORS. All you need to do is:

- Sign up on AWS and access S3 with your IAM credentials
- Launch an EC2 instance and start the web server

How to do it...

First, we configure the CORS configuration to the S3 bucket through the S3 console, and verify that the CORS configuration is applied by putting a JSON file in your S3 bucket and an HTML file in a web server on the EC2 instance. The JSON file named `test.json` holds sample data (`id`, `email`, and `username`) in the JSON format. The HTML file named `index.html` uses JavaScript and retrieves the sample data by sending `XMLHttpRequest` to the JSON file:

1. Sign in to the AWS management console and move to the S3 console at `https://console.aws.amazon.com/s3`.

2. In the S3 console, click on the bucket name, and then click on **Permissions** from the **Properties** tab:

3. Click on **Edit CORS Configuration** on the right-hand side at the bottom:

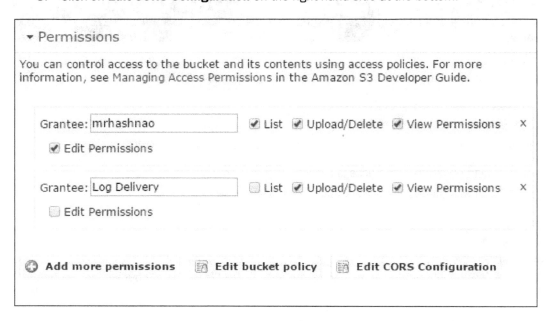

4. Enter the following CORS configuration in the box, and then click on **Save** and **Close** as shown in the following screenshot:

```
<CORSConfiguration>
<CORSRule>
<AllowedOrigin>*</AllowedOrigin>
<AllowedMethod>GET</AllowedMethod>
<AllowedHeader>*</AllowedHeader>
<MaxAgeSeconds>3000</MaxAgeSeconds>
</CORSRule>
</CORSConfiguration>
```

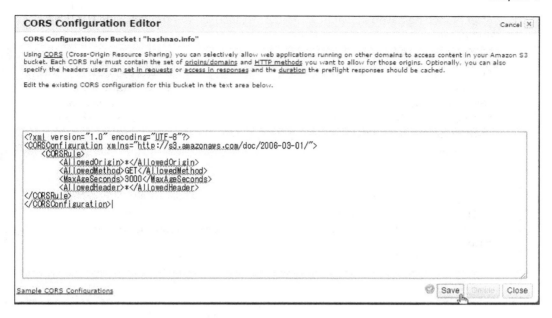

5. Create the following JSON file (from the `<your_bucket>/cors/test.json` path) and put it into your bucket as follows:

```
{
    "id": "xxxx-xxxx-xxxx-xxxx",
    "username": "xxxx",
    "email": "xxx@mail.com"
}
```

You can use any string or number in the JSON file because it is used to load the JSON data from the HTML file, as in the following example:

```
{
    "id": "9561998e-af32-4671-b93e-2a95018de746",
    "username": "hashnao",
    "email": "mrhashnao@gmail.com"
}
```

6. After launching a web server in your EC2 instance, create the following HTML file and put it in your web server. If the document root is /var/www/html, it should be /var/www/html/index.html.

   And, replace your_bucket in the URL http://<your_bucket>/cors/test.json with your bucket name. For example, if you are using a S3 static web site called hashnao.info.s3-website-ap-northeast-1.amazonaws.com, and put the JSON file in the bucket, it should be http://hashnao.info.s3-website-ap-northeast-1.amazonaws.com/cors/test.json:

```html
<!DOCTYPE html>
<html lang="en">
<head>
<meta charset="UTF-8" />
<title>S3 CORS Test</title>
<script type="text/javascript"src="https://ajax.googleapis.com/ajax
/libs/jquery/1.7.2/jquery.min.js" ></script>
<script type="text/javascript">
  $(function(){
    $.ajax({
      type:'GET', contentType:"application/json",
      url:'http://<your_bucket>/cors/test.json',
      error:function(XMLHttpRequest, textStatus,
      errorThrown){
        alert("XMLHttpRequest : " + XMLHttpRequest.status +
        "\n" + "textStatus : " + textStatus + "\n" +
        "errorThrown : " + errorThrown.message);
      },
      success:function(data){
        for(vari in data){
          $("#data").append("<li>"+i+" :
          "+data[i]+"</li>");
        }
      },
      dataType:'json',
      processData: false
    });
  });
</script>
</head>
<body>
<h1>Sample Data</h1>
<ul id="data"></ul>
</form>
</body>
</html>
```

How it works...

As we have finished configuring the CORS configuration and putting the sample JSON and HTML files in the bucket and the web server, we will now verify the sample application. See how the CORS is evaluated, and look into the configuration and the sample file step by step.

After typing the URL where the HTML file is located in the browser, we see the JSON data in the S3 bucket, as shown in the following screenshot:

Sample Data

- id : 9561998e-af32-4671-b93e-2a95018de746
- username : hashnao
- email : mrhashnao@gmail.com

First, let's see the CORS configuration and then verify that the rules in the XML document are evaluated by following the CORS configuration in the previous section.

The CORS configuration consists of an XML document and defines rules with the `CORSRule` element.

 The upper limit of rules you can add to the CORS configuration is 100.

The `CORSRule` element consists of the following optional elements.

The AllowedMethod element

As the name implies, you can use the following values in the `AllowedMethod` element:

- ► `GET`
- ► `PUT`
- ► `POST`
- ► `DELETE`
- ► `HEAD`

The AllowedOrigin element

You can specify the origins that you want to allow cross-origin requests from, for example, `http://yourdomain.com` or `https://yourdomain.com` to enable secure access. In addition, you can use the * wildcard character in the `AllowedOrigin` element, for example, `http://*.yourdomain.com`. If you only use * in the element, it allows all the origins to send cross-origin requests.

The AllowedHeader element

You can specify which request headers to be allowed for a preflight request in the `Access-Control-Request-Headers` header. Amazon S3 will only send the headers allowed in the element.

 For further information about common request headers, see `http://docs.aws.amazon.com/AmazonS3/latest/API/RESTCommonRequestHeaders.html`.

The ExposeHeader element

You can specify which response headers should be allowed access from the customer's application, for example from a JavaScript `XMLHttpRequest` object in the element.

 For further information about common response headers, see `http://docs.aws.amazon.com/AmazonS3/latest/API/RESTCommonResponseHeaders.html`.

The MaxAgeSeconds element

You can specify the time, in seconds, your browser takes to cache the response for a preflight request for the specified resource. The browser does not need to send preflight requests to your S3 bucket by the time defined in the `MaxAgeSeconds` element.

 When performing cross-domain requests, browsers that support CORS will determine if they need to send preflight requests before sending the real headers to the cross-domain servers (here, Amazon S3) in order to determine whether they have permissions to perform the action. For further information about common response headers, see `http://www.w3.org/TR/cors/#cross-origin-request-with-preflight-0`.

Now, let's examine the CORS configuration that we configured in the previous section:

- In the `AllowedOrigin` element, it allows all the origins to access. The syntax is `<AllowedOrigin>*</AllowedOrigin>`.

- In the `AllowedMethod` element, it allows only the GET method to access. The syntax is `<AllowedMethod>GET</AllowedMethod>`.

- In the `AllowedHeader` element, it allows any header to access. The syntax is `<AllowedHeader>*</AllowedHeader>`.

- In the `MaxAgeSeconds` element, it enables 3,000 seconds for caching the response. The syntax is `<MaxAgeSeconds>3000</MaxAgeSeconds>`.

Next, let's take a look at the sample HTML file and see how it sends `XMLHttpRequests` to retrieve and show the JSON data in the bucket.

JavaScript is used in the `script type` tag and the `GET` element is defined in the type element:

```
<script type="text/javascript">
    $(function(){
        $.ajax({
type:'GET',
contentType:"application/json",
```

The `url` element defines the URL where the JSON file is located. If you configure the S3 static web site in the Asia Pacific (Tokyo) Region and put the JSON file in the bucket, the URL should be as follows:

```
url:'http://<your_bucket>/cors/test.json',
```

If the request fails to retrieve the JSON file, it returns the numeric code returned by the server in the `XMLHttpRequest.status` property, the string message in the `textStatus` property, and an error message in the `errorThrown.message` property:

```
error:function(XMLHttpRequest, textStatus, errorThrown){
alert("XMLHttpRequest : " + XMLHttpRequest.status + "\n" +
"textStatus : " + textStatus + "\n" + "errorThrown : " +
errorThrown.message);
},
```

If the request succeeds to retrieve the JSON file, it loads the JSON file and returns a JavaScript object. The `dataType` element evaluates the response as JSON:

```
success:function(data){
for(vari in data){
            $("#data").append("<li>"+i+" : "+data[i]+"</li>");
        }
    },
```

```
dataType:'json',
processData: false
        });
    });
</script>
```

There's more...

As you learned about the CORS configuration and its rules, let's see how the CORS configuration works with the sample JSON file and the HTML file.

Restricting cross-origin requests from a specific domain

If you want to restrict the origin, you can specify the origin in the AllowedOrigin element, for example, http://youdomain.com. The following configuration restricts cross-origin requests only from http://hashnao.info:

```
<CORSConfiguration>
<CORSRule>
<AllowedOrigin>http://hashnao.info</AllowedOrigin>
<AllowedMethod>GET</AllowedMethod>
<MaxAgeSeconds>3000</MaxAgeSeconds>
<AllowedHeader>*</AllowedHeader>
</CORSRule>
</CORSConfiguration>
```

When the sample HTML application sends a cross-origin request to the bucket, it fails and responds, as shown in the following screenshot:

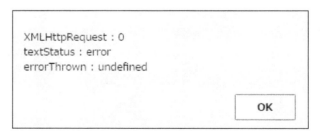

Allowing specific headers for a preflight request

If you want specific headers to be allowed for a preflight request, you can specify the headers in the AllowedHeader element. The following configuration allows Authorization, Accept, Content, and Origin in the request headers:

```
<CORSConfiguration>
<CORSRule>
```

```
<AllowedOrigin>*</AllowedOrigin>
<AllowedMethod>GET</AllowedMethod>
<MaxAgeSeconds>3000</MaxAgeSeconds>
<AllowedHeader>Authorization</AllowedHeader>
<AllowedHeader>Accept</AllowedHeader>
<AllowedHeader>Content-Type</AllowedHeader>
<AllowedHeader>Origin</AllowedHeader>
</CORSRule>
</CORSConfiguration>
```

The preceding configuration succeeds to retrieve and load the JSON file as follows:

Sample Data

- id : 9561998e-af32-4671-b93e-2a95018de746
- username : hashnao
- email : mrhashnao@gmail.com

See also

▶ *Enabling Cross-Origin Resource Sharing*:
http://docs.aws.amazon.com/AmazonS3/latest/dev/cors.html

Walkthrough 2: Enabling CORS with AWS CLI

This section is almost same as walkthrough 1. The difference is that we only use AWS CLI to enable S3 CORS because it is much more simple than operating through S3 console.

Getting ready

You do not have to request permissions to enable S3 CORS. All you need to do is:

▶ Sign up on AWS and be able to access S3 with your IAM credentials

▶ Launch an EC2 instance and start the web server

▶ Install and set up AWS CLI on your PC or use Amazon Linux AMI

How to do it...

To enable CORS with AWS CLI, you just need to create a CORS configuration in the JSON format and use the `aws s3api` command to configure the CORS configuration for your bucket. Let's get started with AWS CLI:

1. Create a CORS configuration file:

```
$ cors=cors_file.json
$ cat> ${cors} <<EOF
{
    "CORSRules": [
        {
            "AllowedHeaders": [
                "Authorization"
            ],
            "MaxAgeSeconds": 3000,
            "AllowedMethods": [
                "GET"
            ],
            "AllowedOrigins": [
                "*"
            ]
        }
    ]
}
EOF
```

2. Configure the CORS configuration for your bucket:

```
$ bucket=your_bucket
$ aws s3api put-bucket-cors \
--bucket ${bucket} \
--cors-configuration file://${cors}
```

How it works...

To verify that the CORS configuration is configured for your bucket, you can use the `get-bucket-cors` subcommand as follows:

```
$ aws s3api get-bucket-cors \
--bucket ${bucket}
{
    "CORSRules": [
        {
```

```
        "AllowedHeaders": [
            "Authorization"
        ],
        "MaxAgeSeconds": 3000,
        "AllowedMethods": [
            "GET"
        ],
        "AllowedOrigins": [
            "*"
        ]
    }
  ]
}
```

There's more...

If you need to delete the CORS configuration, you can use the `delete-bucket-cors` subcommand as follows:

```
$ aws s3api delete-bucket-cors \
--bucket ${bucket}
```

See also

▸   AWS CLI S3 API: *put-bucket-cors* http://docs.aws.amazon.com/cli/latest/ reference/s3api/put-bucket-cors.html

10
Managing Object Lifecycle to Lower the Cost

In this chapter, you will learn:

- ► How to apply the lifecycle policy through the S3 console
- ► How to apply the lifecycle policy with AWS CLI

Introduction

Amazon S3 allows users to manage objects' lifecycles in order to lower the cost of S3 objects that should be removed in a certain period, archive log files that should be stored for backup, or auditing in the future. For example, you can configure a lifecycle policy to automatically delete objects in a week because the objects are a collection of data to create reports and are not needed anymore after that. Otherwise you can archive objects into Amazon Glacier in a month because the objects are system log files, which need not be examined immediately for auditing but need to be examined in a couple of days when it's needed. In addition, Amazon S3 supports versioning so that you can create a lifecycle configuration to keep several versions of objects.

 Amazon Glacier is a low-cost storage service for archiving and online backup. For further information about Amazon Glacier, see http://aws.amazon.com/glacier/.

The following are the situations in which you might want to use lifecycle management:

- ▶ You have a bucket to store log files and you want to automatically archive log files into Glacier in a certain time after the creation and then delete the archived objects
- ▶ You have a bucket to store your contents and want to automatically retain the current version as a previous version in a certain time after the contents have been updated

You can configure a lifecycle policy on your bucket using the Amazon S3 console or the Amazon S3 API. The following methods are currently supported to configure a lifecycle policy:

- ▶ The Amazon S3 console
- ▶ AWS SDK for Java
- ▶ AWS SDK for .NET
- ▶ AWS SDK for Ruby
- ▶ AWS SDK for Python
- ▶ AWS SDK for PHP
- ▶ REST API
- ▶ AWS CLI

How to apply the lifecycle policy through the S3 console

This section introduces the process of configuring lifecycle rules based on a couple of scenarios and how the rules work checking the storage class with AWS CLI.

Getting ready

You do not have to request permissions to configure the lifecycle policy over your bucket. All you need to do is:

- ▶ Sign up on AWS and be able to access S3 with your IAM credentials
- ▶ Enable server access logging for your bucket

How to do it...

To enable the lifecycle of objects, you need to create a lifecycle policy, specify where to apply the whole bucket (or a specific prefix) and the lifetime (in days). We will configure a lifecycle policy with the following parameters:

- ▶ **Apply the Rule to** (Where): `logs/`

- ▶ **Permanently Delete** (Lifetime): 1 day
- ▶ **Rule Name** (Optional): `del_logs`

Next, let's create the lifecycle policy, configure it to the bucket, and then verify that the policy is configured to the bucket through the S3 console:

1. First, sign in to the AWS management console and move to the S3 console at `https://console.aws.amazon.com/s3`.

2. Enable S3 access logging to your bucket following the instructions under *How to enable and manage S3 server access logging* from *Chapter 2, Hosting a Static Website on Amazon S3 Bucket*.

3. In the S3 console, click on the bucket name. Select **Lifecycle** and then click on **Add rule** from the **Properties** panel:

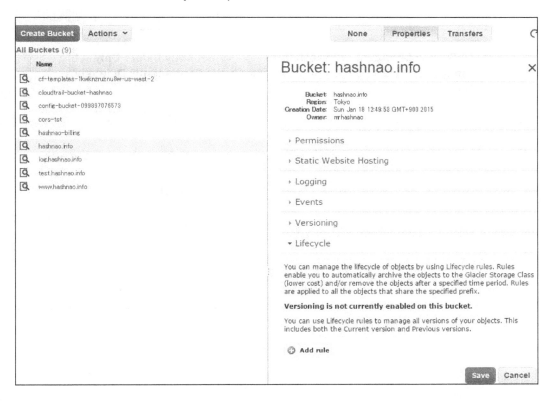

4. In the **Step 1: Choose Rule Target** section, select **A Prefix** and input `logs/` in the box, and then click on **Configure Rule >**:

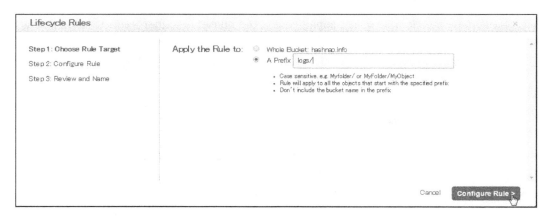

5. In the **Step 2: Configure Rule** section, select **Permanently Delete Only** in the **Action on Objects** box and input the number in the **Permanently Delete** box and click on **Review >**:

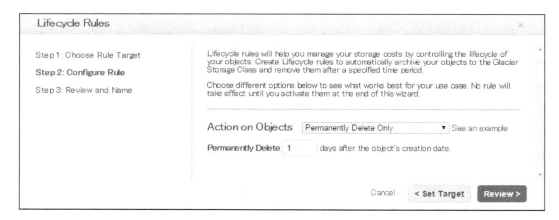

6. In the **Rule Name** box, input your rule name, review the parameters, and then click on **Save Rule**:

7. Confirm that the **Enabled** box is enabled as shown in the following screenshot:

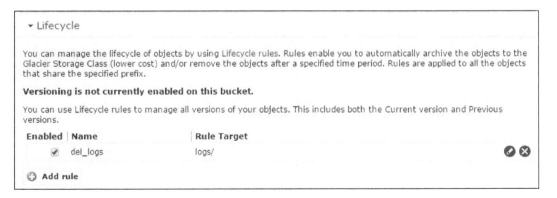

How it works...

As we configured the lifecycle policy to a bucket, we need to check how the policy works. To verify that your lifecycle policy is enabled, you need to simply see that the objects are deleted in 1 day after the objects (server access log files) are created through the S3 console.

You can also find out whether an object is scheduled to expire by checking the **Expiry Date and Expiation Rule** field through the S3 console or using the GET object or the HEAD object APIs. The following screenshot shows that the **Expiry Date** and **Expiration Rule** have been enabled from the properties panel in the S3 console:

Object: 2015-03-30-01-40-46-FB6DD66BB8DEDA0C

Bucket:	hashnao.info
Folder:	logs
Name:	2015-03-30-01-40-46-FB6DD66BB8DEDA0C
Link:	https://s3-ap-northeast-1.amazonaws.com/hashnao.info/logs/2015-03-30-01-40-46-FB6DD66BB8DEDA0C
Size:	286
Last Modified:	Mon Mar 30 10:40:48 GMT+900 2015
Owner:	s3-log-service
ETag:	a83f9570f097b17059a30bd8ed28e838
Expiry Date:	Wed Apr 01 09:00:00 GMT+900 2015
Expiration Rule:	del_logs

There's more...

As we tried configuring a sample lifecycle policy through the S3 console, we will configure more practical lifecycle policies.

Walkthrough – applying several lifecycle policies

We are planning to create a bucket to store several kinds of log files (for example, application server and web server access) for each prefix and archive the log files applying different lifecycle policies.

The policies of the application server are as follows:

- **Apply the Rule to** (Where): `logs/ap/`
- **Action on Current Version: Archive Only**
    - **Archive to the Glacier Storage Class**: 30 days
- **Action on Previous Versions: Permanently Delete Only**
    - **Permanently Delete**: 60 days
- **Rule Name** (Optional): `logs_ap`

Amazon S3 provides a storage class for each object. When objects are uploaded, they are defined as the standard storage class by default. The Glacier storage class is primarily used for archival purpose. For further information, see `http://docs.amazonaws.cn/en_us/ AmazonS3/latest/dev/object-archival.html/`.

The policies of a web server are as follows:

- **Apply the Rule to** (Where): `logs/web/`
- **Action on Current Version: Archive Only**
    - **Archive to the Glacier Storage Class**: `30` days
- **Action on Previous Versions: Permanently Delete Only**
    - **Permanently Delete**: `60` days
- **Rule Name** (Optional): `logs_web`

The following diagram shows the lifecycle policies:

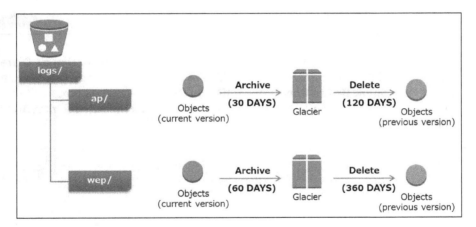

Let's try to understand the preceding diagram in detail:

- The objects under both `logs/ap/` and `logs/web/` were uploaded to the bucket on January 1
- For the `logs/ap/` prefix, the lifecycle takes effect on January 1 (30 days after the object was created) and the object is automatically archived to the Glacier object class
- For the `logs/ap/` prefix, the lifecycle takes effect on March 2 (60 days after the object was created) and the previous version is permanently deleted
- For the `logs/web/` prefix, the lifecycle takes effect on March 2 (60 days after the object was created) and the object is automatically archived to the Glacier object class

▶ For the `logs/web/` prefix, the lifecycle takes effect on May 1 (120 days after the object was created) and the previous version is permanently deleted

Next, let's create the lifecycle policy, configure it to the bucket, and then verify that the policy is configured to the bucket through the S3 console:

1. Open the lifecycle configurations panel, follow the steps from 1 to 3 of the *How to do it...* section.

2. In the **Step 1: Choose Rule Target** section, select **A Prefix** and input `logs/ap/` in the box, and then click on **Configure Rule >**.

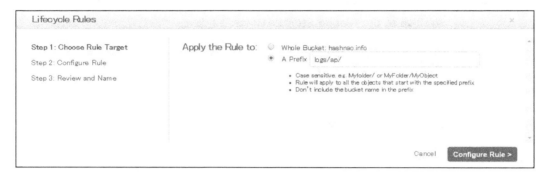

3. In the **Step 2: Configure Rule** section, select **Archive Only** in the **Action on Current Version** box, input the number in the **Archive to the Glacier Storage Class** box, and select **Permanent Delete Only** in the **Action on Previous Versions** box. Input the number in the **Permanently Delete** box, and check the **I acknowledge that Archive...** box, and then, click on **Review >**:

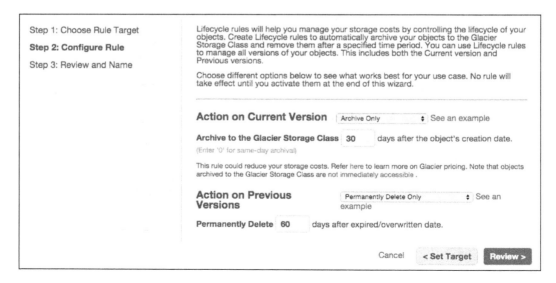

4. In the **Rule Name** box, input your rule name, review the parameters, and then click on **Create and Activate Rule**:

5. Configure the lifecycle policy for the `logs/web/` prefix in the same way.

6. Confirm that the **Enabled** box is enabled as shown in the following screenshot:

After configuring your lifecycle policy and after the objects are applied with your lifecycle policy, you can confirm that the objects are archived in the storage class through both the S3 console and the AWS CLI `s3api` subcommand as follows.

You can see the storage class of objects in the **Details** section in the **Properties** panel in the S3 console, as shown in the following screenshot:

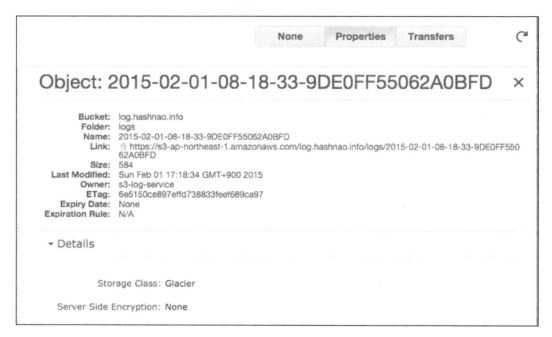

You can also check the storage class in the `StorageClass` key with the `aws s3api` subcommand as follows:

```
$ bucket="your_bucket"
$ key="logs/"
$ aws s3api list-objects --bucket ${bucket} --prefix ${key}  \
--query \
'Contents[].{Key: Key, StorageClass: StorageClass, LastModified:
LastModified }'}
```

If the lifecycle policy is applied and the object is archived into Glacier, you can see the storage class is Glacier in the `StorageClass` key, as shown in the following output:

```
[
    {
        "LastModified": "2015-02-01T08:18:34.000Z",
        "StorageClass": "GLACIER",
```

```
        "Key": "logs/2015-02-01-08-18-33-9DE0FF55062A0BFD"
    }
]
```

Applying lifecycle configuration rules

If you add a lifecycle configuration to a bucket, the configuration rules apply to both existing objects and objects that are created or added later after you add the rules. For example, if you add a configuration rule to delete a specific prefix (for example, `logs/`) in 7 days, today, Amazon S3 will queue, for deleting, any existing objects created 7 days ago.

In addition, there is usually some lag for a few minutes before a new or updated lifecycle configuration is fully transmitted to all the Amazon S3 systems when you add a lifecycle configuration to a bucket. The delay can occur when you delete a lifecycle configuration as well.

Object expiration for versioning and server access logging

If you have your bucket nonversioned, Amazon S3 permanently deletes the object. This is called the `Expiration` action.

On the other hand, if you have your bucket versioning enabled, Amazon S3 logically deletes the current version object adding a delete as the new current version. It is called the `NoncurrentVersionExpiration` action and permanently deletes the noncurrent versions.

If you have server access logging enabled, when an object is permanently deleted, Amazon S3 records the permanent removal in the logging adding `S3.EXPIRE.OBJECT`.

If you have your bucket versioning enabled, when an object is logically deleted, Amazon S3 records the permanent removal in the logging adding `S3.CREATE.DELETEMARKER`.

The Glacier storage class

You can use the `Glacier` storage class to the existing objects configuring lifecycle policy. However, you cannot assign the `Glacier` storage class, when you upload your objects to the bucket, nor can you access the archived objects through the Amazon Glacier console or the API. You can access the archived objects only through the Amazon S3 console or the API. This is because the archived objects are Amazon S3 objects.

See also

- ▸ *Object Lifecycle Management* http://docs.aws.amazon.com/AmazonS3/latest/dev/object-lifecycle-mgmt.html
- ▸ *Specifying a Lifecycle Configuration* http://docs.aws.amazon.com/AmazonS3/latest/dev/how-to-set-lifecycle-configuration-intro.html
- ▸ *Object Expiration* http://docs.aws.amazon.com/AmazonS3/latest/dev/ObjectExpiration.html

How to apply the lifecycle policy with AWS CLI

This section follows the same step in the previous section, but the difference is to use AWS CLI to apply a lifecycle rule. The advantage is that it is able to manage a lifecycle policy file in JSON format.

Getting ready

You do not have to request permissions to configure lifecycle policy over your bucket. All you need to do is:

▸ Sign up on AWS and be able to access S3 with your IAM credentials

▸ Enable Server Access Logging to your bucket

How to do it...

To enable the lifecycle of objects using AWS CLI, you need to create a lifecycle policy in the JSON format and use the `aws s3api` subcommand to configure the lifecycle policy for you bucket. We are configuring the same policy used in the previous section. Now, let's start to create the policy with AWS CLI:

1. Create a lifecycle policy file:

    ```
    $ policy=lifecycle_policy.json
    $ cat> ${policy} <<EOF
    {
        "Rules": [
            {
                "Status": "Enabled",
                "Prefix": "logs/",
                "Expiration": {
                    "Days": 1
                },
                "ID": "del_logs"
            }
        ]
    }
    EOF
    ```

2. Update the AWS config file entering the IAM credentials:

    ```
    $ bucket=your-bucket-name
    $ aws s3api put-bucket-lifecycle \
    --bucket=$bucket \
    --lifecycle-configuration file://${policy}
    ```

How it works...

To verify that the lifecycle policy is configured for your bucket, you can use the `get-bucket-lifecycle` subcommand as follows:

```
$ aws s3api get-bucket-lifecycle \
--bucket=$bucket
{
    "Rules": [
        {
            "Status": "Enabled",
            "Prefix": "logs/",
            "Expiration": {
                "Days": 1
            },
            "ID": "del_logs"
        }
    ]
}
```

To delete the lifecycle policy, you can use the `delete-bucket-lifecycle` subcommand as follows. However, the subcommand deletes all the lifecycle policies, if you configured several lifecycle polices for a bucket:

```
$ aws s3api delete-bucket-lifecycle \
--bucket=$bucket
```

There's more...

As we tried configuring a sample lifecycle policy using AWS CLI, we will configure more practical lifecycle policies.

Walkthrough – archiving the current version into Glacier and deleting the previous versions

We are planning to create a bucket and enable versioning for the bucket, and configure the following lifecycle policy:

- **Apply the Rule to** (Where): **Whole bucket**
- **Action on Current Version: Archive and then Expire**
    - **Archive to the Glacier Storage Class**: 60 days
    - **Expire**: 120 days (after the object was created)

- **Action on Previous Versions**: Permanently Delete Only

  - **Permanently Delete**: 360 days

The following diagram shows the lifecycle policy:

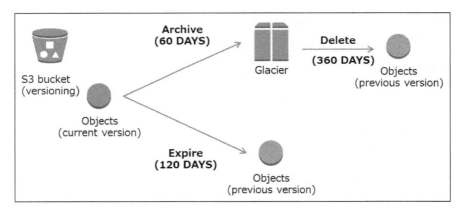

Let's try to understand the preceding diagram in detail:

- The object was uploaded to the bucket on January 1
- The lifecycle takes effect on March 2 (60 days after the object was created) and the object is automatically archived to the Glacier object class
- The lifecycle takes effect again on May 1 (120 days after the object was created) and the object automatically expires
- The expired current version is retained as the previous version as versioning is enabled on the bucket
- The lifecycle takes effect on December 27 (360 days after the object was created) and the previous version is permanently deleted

Next, let's see the lifecycle policy, configure it to the bucket, and then verify that the policy is configured to the bucket:

1. Create a lifecycle policy file:

```
$ policy=lifecycle_policy.json
$ cat> ${policy} <<EOF
{
    "Rules": [
        {
            "Status": "Enabled",
            "NoncurrentVersionExpiration": {
                "NoncurrentDays": 360
            },
```

```
            "Transition": {
                "Days": 60,
                "StorageClass": "GLACIER"
            },
            "Prefix": "",
            "Expiration": {
                "Days": 120
            },
            "ID": "archive_policy"
        }
    ]
}
EOF
```

2. Configure the lifecycle policy to the bucket:

```
$ bucket=your-bucket-name
$ aws s3api put-bucket-lifecycle \
--bucket=$bucket \
--lifecycle-configuration file://${policy}
```

3. Verify that the lifecycle policy is configured with the `get-bucket-lifecycle` subcommand:

```
$ aws s3api get-bucket-lifecycle \
--bucket=$bucket \
{
    "Rules": [
        {
            "Status": "Enabled",
            "NoncurrentVersionExpiration": {
                "NoncurrentDays": 360
            },
            "Transition": {
                "Days": 60,
                "StorageClass": "GLACIER"
            },
            "Prefix": "",
            "Expiration": {
                "Days": 120
            },
            "ID": "archive_policy"
        }
    ]
}
```

Archival storage charges

Amazon Glacier is suitable to archive your objects in order to achieve lifecycle management and reduce storage costs. We configured the lifecycle policy using the `GLACIER` storage class to archive objects at *Walkthrough – Archiving current version into Glacier and delete previous versions*.

On the other hand, you should consider how the Glacier storage is charged in order to know if it is appropriate for your environment and properly use the `GLACIER` storage class:

- ▶ Amazon S3 uses 8 KB storage for the name of the object and other metadata for each object archived to Amazon Glacier, in order to retrieve a real-time list of the archived objects using the Amazon S3 API. The additional 8 KB storage is charged for each archived object in the standard Amazon S3 rates.

- ▶ Amazon Glacier adds 32 KB of storage for indexing and related metadata for each archived object in order to identify and restore the archived objects. The additional 32 KB storage is charged for each archived object in the Amazon Glacier rates.

Let's assume you archived 1 GB of 10,000 objects in the US Standard region for three months, the archive pricing will be calculated as follows:

- ▶ *1.000032 GB * 10,000 objects= 10,000.32 GB* of the Amazon Glacier storage
- ▶ *0.000008 * 10,000 objects= 0.08 GB* of the Amazon S3 Standard storage

Then, the total will be:

- ▶ *(10,000.32 GB* 3 months * $0.0100) + (0.08 GB * 3 months* $0.0300) = $300.017*

The following table also shows the formula of how to calculate the archive pricing:

	Size (GB)	Object	Total (GB)	Price	Months	Sub Total
Glacier	1.000032	10,000	10000.32	$0.0100	3	$300.010
S3	0.000008	10,000	0.08	$0.0300	3	$0.007
					Total	**$300.017**

- ▶ Deleting the objects archived to Amazon Glacier is free if they are archived for 3 months or later. However, the deletion fee is charged for items deleted prior to 90 days. If you delete 1 GB of data in 1 month after uploading it, you will be charged for 2 months of Amazon Glacier Storage. The prorated charge is $0.03 per GB.

- ▶ An archive request to transit your objects to the GLACIER storage is charged. (Glacier Archive and Restore Requests: $0.05 per 1,000 requests in the U.S. Standard region)

- ▶ You can restore up to 5 percent of your archived data for free, each month from Amazon Glacier.

Let's assume you have 100 TB of archived data on a given day in Amazon Glacier, you can restore up to 167 GB for free that day (assuming it is a 30-day month):

▶   *100 TB (1,024 GB * 100) * 5% / 30 days = 170 GB*

The data restore charge is calculated at the peak billable restore rate in GB/hour for the entire month.

While you can restore up to 5 percent of your archived data for free each month, you can restore your archived data more quickly by paying an additional charge. Let's look at the following examples to calculate the data restore charge:

Example 1: Archiving 100 TB of data to Amazon Glacier and restoring 200 GB in 4 hours.

First, we need to calculate the peak restore rate. The peak restore rate is 200 GB/4 hours and 50 GB/hour.

Next is the peak billable restore rate. We need to subtract the amount of data for free from the peak rate. The free data is 170 GB/4 hours or 43 GB per hour. Finally, the peak billable restore rate is 7 GB per hour (the amounts of data for free: 50 GB/hour - the peak rate: 43 GB/hour).

Then, we calculate how much we need to pay. We need to multiply the peak billable restore rate (7 GB per hour) by the data restore fee ($0.01/GB) by the number of hours in a month (720 hours). The charge is calculated as follows:

▶   *7 GB/hour * $0.01 * 720 hours = $52.80*

Example 2: Archiving 100 TB of data to Amazon Glacier and restoring 200 GB in 8 hours.

The peak restore rate is 200 GB/8 hours and 25 GB per hour.

The free data is 170 GB/8 hours or 21 GB per hour. Finally, the peak billable restore rate is 4 GB per hour (the amounts of data for free: 25 GB/hour - the peak rate: 21 GB/hour).

Then, we calculate how much we need to pay. We need to multiply the peak billable restore rate (4 GB per hour) by the data restore fee ($0.01/GB) by the number of hours in a month (720 hours). The charge is calculated as follows:

▶   *4 GB/hour * $0.01 * 720 hours = $26.40*

Example 3: Archiving 100 TB of data to Amazon Glacier and restoring 200 GB in 28 hours.

The data restore fee is not charged if you restore your archived data over 28 hours because the daily free restore allowance would no longer exceed.

See also...

- ▸ *AWS CLI s3api: put-bucket-lifecycle* http://docs.aws.amazon.com/cli/
  latest/reference/s3api/put-bucket-lifecycle.html
- ▸ *Lifecycle Configuration Elements* http://docs.aws.amazon.com/AmazonS3/
  latest/dev/intro-lifecycle-rules.html
- ▸ *Object Archival* https://docs.aws.amazon.com/AmazonS3/latest/dev/
  object-archival.html

11

S3 Performance Optimization

Amazon S3 is a highly-scalable, reliable, and low-latency data storage service at a very low cost, designed for mission-critical and primary data storage. It provides the Amazon S3 APIs to simplify your programming tasks.

Since you learned how to operate the Amazon S3 API using AWS SDKs, deploy a static site on Amazon S3, secure S3 bucket, calculate Amazon S3 cost, and so on through the previous chapters, we will now be focusing on how to optimize S3 performance in this chapter.

S3 performance optimization is composed of several factors, for example, which region to choose to reduce latency, considering the naming scheme and optimizing the put and get operations. In this chapter, you will learn:

- ▸ How to optimize PUT requests
- ▸ How to optimize GET requests

Introduction

Before getting into the details of S3 performance optimization, let's quickly look at the factors of S3 performance optimization in order to improve understanding.

Choosing a region to optimize latency

Amazon S3 provides service to several regions around the world, so you can choose any region that is geographically close to your environment to optimize the latency for getting and putting objects. For example, if you are planning to launch your service in Singapore, you can choose the Asia Pacific (Singapore) region.

On the other hand, if you need to minimize cost, you can compare the storage pricing, the request pricing, and the data transfer pricing between the regions and choose the region that is suitable to your requirements.

> You also need to consider the location keeping in mind the local law as well as the latency, depending on what kind of data you want to store or what kind of customers you want to deal with. For example, if you intend to store data that needs to be geographically located in a specific region or country, you need to choose a specific region depending on the local law.

Some of the regions are listed as follows:

- ▸ US Standard
- ▸ US West (Oregon)
- ▸ US West (N. California)
- ▸ EU (Ireland)
- ▸ EU (Frankfurt)
- ▸ Asia Pacific (Singapore)
- ▸ Asia Pacific (Tokyo)
- ▸ Asia Pacific (Sydney)
- ▸ South America (Sao Paulo)

You can see the preceding regions marked in the following map:

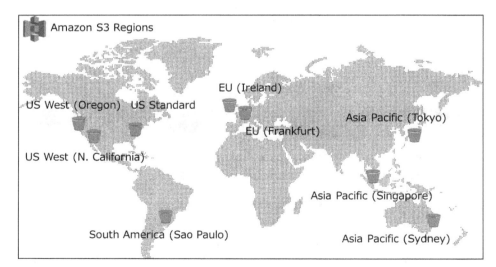

If you choose the US standard region, you can use the following two endpoints:

- ► s3.amazonaws.com (N. Virginia or Pacific Northwest)
- ► s3-external-1.amazonaws.com (N. Virginia only)

For more information about the Amazon S3 regions, see `http://docs.aws.amazon.com/general/latest/gr/rande.html#s3_region`.

 The AWS China (Beijing) region is under the limited preview. For more information, see `http://www.amazonaws.cn/en/`.

The data consistency model

Amazon S3 provides an eventual consistency for requests and does not currently support object locking. Amazon S3 never adds partial objects, so if you send a PUT request to your bucket and receive a success response, Amazon S3 adds the entire object to the bucket. In addition, if you send a PUT request to an existing key, a GET request after the PUT request might return the old object or the updated object, but it will never overwrite corrupted or partial data to the object key.

Another example is that, if you send two PUT requests to the same key at the same time, the request with the latest time stamp is processed. This is because updates are key-based and it is not possible to make atomic updates across keys. If you need an object-locking system to secure the consistency, you need to design and create the object-locking system, and integrate it into your application layer or use versioning instead.

Regarding supported consistency, the US standard region supports all requests and all other regions except US standard support read-after-write consistency for PUT requests and eventual consistency to overwrite the PUT and DELETE requests.

 For more information about PUT requests, see `http://docs.aws.amazon.com/AmazonS3/latest/API/RESTObjectPUT.html`.

Key naming schema

If you need 100 PUT/LIST/DELETE requests per second or over 300 GET request per second in an S3 bucket, you need to consider not redistributing key names. In addition, it is recommended to open a support case and ask for the support if the workload is expected to exceed 300 PUT/LIST/DELETE requests per second or over 800 GET request per second for a surge request.

There are two options to support high request rates based on the kind of workloads:

- ▶ Workloads that consist of a mix of requests types: Choosing appropriate key names will ensure better performance regardless of the number of requests per second by providing low-latency access to the Amazon S3 index.

- ▶ Workloads of intensive GET: It is recommended to use CloudFront to reduce the number of GETs request to the Amazon S3 bucket if your request consists of a large number of GETs.

If you routinely process over 100 requests per second, the guideline will apply. However, if your typical workloads occasionally contain bursts of 100 requests per second and less than 800 requests per second, it is not necessary to follow this instruction.

For example, when you need to upload a large number of objects, you might choose the key name with some combination of the date and unique ID in the prefix, as shown in the following diagram. This brings a performance problem.

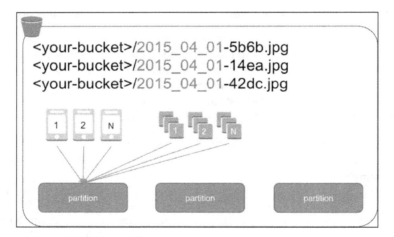

This is because Amazon S3 holds an index of object key names in each AWS region and object keys are stored lexicographically across multiple partitions in the index. If you use a sequential prefix, for example, a timestamp or alphabetical sequence, it increases the likelihood that a large number of the keys are stored in a partition and overwhelms the I/O capacity of the partition. On the other hand, it is able to increase the likelihood of distributing key names across multiple index partitions, if you add a random prefix to the key names, as shown in the following diagram:

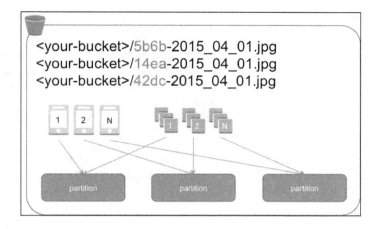

```
<your-bucket>/5b6b-2015_04_01.jpg
<your-bucket>/14ea-2015_04_01.jpg
<your-bucket>/42dc-2015_04_01.jpg
```

Now, let's see the examples of how to introduce randomness in the prefix:

- Add a hex hash string as a prefix to the key name. It is recommended to add a hex hash to the key name prefix, for example by using the MD5 hash. It is sufficient to add three or four characters in the prefix as follows:

```
<your-bucket>/2015_04_01-5b6b-0733.jpg
<your-bucket>/2015_04_01-14ea-7259.jpg

<your-bucket>/5b6b-0733-2015_04_01.jpg
<your-bucket>/14ea-7259-2015_04_01.jpg
```

- Reverse the key name string. If you choose to use an increasing sequence of the application ID in the prefix, you can avoid overwhelming a single index partition by reversing the application ID, for example:

```
<your-bucket>/09881986/20150401_001122.jpg
<your-bucket>/09881986/20150401_001132.jpg
<your-bucket>/09881987/20150401_001222.jpg
<your-bucket>/09881988/20150401_002122.jpg

<your-bucket>/68918890/20150401_001122.jpg
<your-bucket>/68918890/20150401_001132.jpg
<your-bucket>/78918890/20150401_001222.jpg
<your-bucket>/78918890/20150401_002122.jpg
```

CloudHarmony for measuring S3 performance

CloudHarmony (`https://cloudharmony.com/`) provides research and the comparison of cloud providers and their services, for example, the performance analytics and reports of several Cloud providers including Amazon Web Services as well. If you want to measure S3 performance to choose an appropriate region for your environment, for example, by measuring bandwidth for downloading your objects and latency, CloudHarmony will definitely be of help.

CloudHarmony provides the following services: CloudSquare, CoudScores, CloudReports, and CloudMatch. Here, we will see the services that will help us understand the Amazon S3 performance:

> ▶ **CloudSquare** (`https://cloudharmony.com/cloudsquare`): CloudSquare provides service information about a cloud provider and their services, for example, when it comes to Amazon S3, it shows the S3 regions, SLA report, the storage pricing, the bandwidth pricing, and so on. CloudSquare also provides the service status of the Cloud providers' services. The following screenshot shows the service availability of Amazon S3 in the last six months:

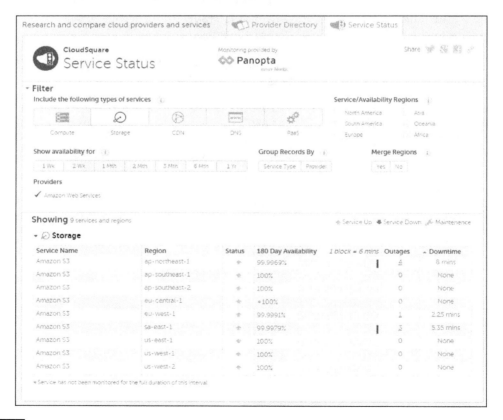

▶ **CloudMatch** (`https://cloudharmony.com/speedtest`): The CloudMatch Amazon Web Services Speed test provides speed tests for downlink, uplink and latency of Amazon S3. You can choose the test types (downlink, uplink, latency, and DNS), specify the test duration (the number of tests, seconds, and minutes), and the test protocols (HTTP, HTTPS). After configuring the test options, the test automatically begins, and the test results will be generated in a few minutes, as shown in the following screenshot:

As you have already learned the Amazon S3 regions and the Amazon S3 data consistency model, let's see how to optimize S3 performance.

How to optimize PUT requests

To optimize PUT requests, it would be effective to use multipart uploads because it can aggregate throughput by parallelizing PUT requests and uploading a large object into parts. It is recommended that the size of each part should be between 25 and 50 MB for higher networks and 10 MB for mobile networks.

Multipart upload consists of three-step processes; the first step is initiating the upload, next is uploading the object parts, and finally, after uploading all the parts, the multipart upload is finished. The following methods are currently supported to upload objects with multipart upload:

- ▶ AWS SDK for Android
- ▶ AWS SDK for iOS
- ▶ AWS SDK for Java
- ▶ AWS SDK for JavaScript
- ▶ AWS SDK for PHP
- ▶ AWS SDK for Python
- ▶ AWS SDK for Ruby
- ▶ AWS SDK for .NET
- ▶ REST API
- ▶ AWS CLI

In order to try multipart upload and see how much it aggregates throughput, we use AWS SDK for Node.js and S3 via NPM (package manager for Node.js).

 AWS CLI also supports multipart upload. When you use the AWS CLI s3 or s3api subcommand to upload an object, the object is automatically uploaded via multipart requests.

Getting ready

You need to complete the following set up in advance:

- ▶ Sign up on AWS and be able to access S3 with your IAM credentials
- ▶ Install and set up AWS CLI in your PC or use Amazon Linux AMI
- ▶ Install Node.js following the instructions in, *Learning AWS SDK for Node.js and basic S3 operations with sample code* in *Chapter 1, Managing Common Operations with AWS SDKs*

It is recommended that you score the benchmark from your local PC or if you use the EC2 instance, you should launch an instance and create an S3 bucket in different regions. For example, if you launch an instance in the Asia Pacific Tokyo region, you should create an S3 bucket in the US standard region. The reason is that the latency between EC2 and S3 is very low, and it is hard to see the difference.

How to do it...

We upload a 300 GB file in an S3 bucket over HTTP in two ways; one is to use a multipart upload and the other is not to use multipart upload to compare the time. To clearly see how the performance differs, I launched an instance and created an S3 bucket in different regions as follows:

▸ **EC2 instance**: Asia Pacific Tokyo Region (ap-northeast-1)

▸ **S3 bucket**: US Standard region (us-east-1)

First, we install the S3 Node.js module via npm, create a dummy file, upload the object into a bucket using a sample Node.js script without enabling multipart upload, and then do the same enabling multipart upload, so that we can see how multipart upload performs the operation. Now, let's move on to the instructions:

1. Install s3 via the npm command:

```
$ cd aws-nodejs-sample/
$ npm install s3
```

2. Create a 300 GB dummy file:

```
$ file=300mb.dmp
$ dd if=/dev/zero of=${file} bs=10M count=30
```

3. Put the following script and save the script as s3_upload.js:

```
// Load the SDK
var AWS = require('aws-sdk');
var s3 = require('s3');
var conf = require('./conf');

// Load parameters
var client = s3.createClient({
  maxAsyncS3: conf.maxAsyncS3,
  s3RetryCount: conf.s3RetryCount,
  s3RetryDelay: conf.s3RetryDelay,
  multipartUploadThreshold: conf.multipartUploadThreshold,
```

```
      multipartUploadSize: conf.multipartUploadSize,
    });

    var params = {
      localFile: conf.localFile,

      s3Params: {
        Bucket: conf.Bucket,
        Key: conf.localFile,
      },
    };

    // upload objects
    console.log("## s3 Parameters");
    console.log(conf);

    console.log("## Begin uploading.");
    var uploader = client.uploadFile(params);
    uploader.on('error', function(err) {
      console.error("Unable to upload:", err.stack);
    });
    uploader.on('progress', function() {
      console.log("Progress",
    uploader.progressMd5Amount,uploader.progressAmount,
    uploader.progressTotal);
    });
    uploader.on('end', function() {
      console.log("## Finished uploading.");
    });
```

4. Create a configuration file and save the file conf.js in the same directory as s3_
    upload.js:

```
    exports.maxAsyncS3 = 20;         // default value
    exports.s3RetryCount = 3;        // default value
    exports.s3RetryDelay = 1000;     // default value
    exports.multipartUploadThreshold = 20971520;    // default
    value
    exports.multipartUploadSize = 15728640;          // default
    value
    exports.Bucket = "your-bucket-name";
    exports.localFile = "300mb.dmp";
    exports.Key = "300mb.dmp";
```

How it works...

First of all, let's try uploading a 300 GB object using multipart upload, and then upload the same file without using multipart upload.

You can upload an object and see how long it takes by typing the following command:

```
$ time node s3_upload.js
## s3 Parameters
{ maxAsyncS3: 20,
  s3RetryCount: 3,
  s3RetryDelay: 1000,
  multipartUploadThreshold: 20971520,
  multipartUploadSize: 15728640,
  localFile: './300mb.dmp',
  Bucket: 'bucket-sample-us-east-1',
  Key: './300mb.dmp' }
## Begin uploading.
Progress 0 16384 314572800
Progress 0 32768 314572800
...
Progress 0 314572800 314572800
Progress 0 314572800 314572800
## Finished uploading.

real    0m16.111s
user    0m4.164s
sys     0m0.884s
```

As it took about 16 seconds to upload the object, the transfer rate was 18.75 MB/sec.

Then, let's change the following parameters in the configuration (conf.js) as follows and see the result. The 300 GB object is uploaded through only one S3 client and

```
    exports.maxAsyncS3 = 1;
    exports. multipartUploadThreshold = 2097152000;

    exports.maxAsyncS3 = 1;
    exports.s3RetryCount = 3;        // default value
    exports.s3RetryDelay = 1000;     // default value
    exports.multipartUploadThreshold = 2097152000;
    exports.multipartUploadSize = 15728640;          // default value
    exports.Bucket = "your-bucket-name";
    exports.localFile = "300mb.dmp";
    exports.Key = "300mb.dmp";
```

Let's see the result after changing the parameters in the configuration (`conf.js`):

```
$ time node s3_upload.js
## s3 Parameters
...
## Begin uploading.
Progress 0 16384 314572800
...
Progress 0 314572800 314572800
## Finished uploading.

real    0m41.887s
user    0m4.196s
sys     0m0.728s
```

As it took about 42 seconds to upload the object, the transfer rate was 7.14 MB/sec.

Now, let's quickly check each parameter, and then get to the conclusion;

- ▶ `maxAsyncS3` defines the maximum number of simultaneous requests that S3 clients are open to Amazon S3. The default value is 20.

- ▶ `s3RetryCount` defines the number of retries when a request fails. The default value is 3.

- ▶ `s3RetryDelay` is how many milliseconds S3 clients will wait when a request fails. The default value is 1000.

- ▶ `multipartUploadThreshold` defines the size of uploading objects via multipart requests. The object will be uploaded via multipart request, if you choose an object that is greater than the size you specified. The default value is 20 MB, the minimum is 5 MB, and the maximum is 5 GB.

- ▶ `multipartUploadSize` defines the size for each part when uploaded via the multipart request. The default value is 15 MB, the minimum is 5 MB, and the maximum is 5 GB.

The following table shows the speed test score with different parameters:

maxAsyncS3	1	20	20	40	30
s3RetryCount	3	3	3	3	3
s3RetryDelay	1000	1000	1000	1000	1000
multipartUploadThreshold	2097152000	20971520	20971520	20971520	20971520
multipartUploadSize	15728640	15728640	31457280	15728640	10728640
Time (seconds)	41.88	16.11	17.41	16.37	9.68
Transfer Rate (MB)	7.51	19.53	18.07	19.22	32.50

In conclusion, multipart upload is effective for optimizing the PUT operation, aggregating throughput. However, you need to consider the following:

▶ Benchmark your scenario and evaluate the number of retry count, delay, parts, and the multipart upload size based on the networks that your application belongs to.

There's more...

Multipart upload specification

There are limits to using multipart upload. The following table shows the specification of multipart upload:

Item	Specification
Maximum object size	5 TB
Maximum number of parts per upload	10,000
Part numbers	1 to 10,000 (inclusive)
Part size	5 MB to 5 GB, last part can be more than 5 MB
Maximum number of parts returned for a list of parts request	1,000
Maximum number of multipart uploads returned in a list of multipart uploads request	1,000

Multipart upload and charging

If you initiate multipart upload and abort the request, Amazon S3 deletes the upload artifacts and any parts you have uploaded and you are not charged for the bills. However, you are charged for all storage, bandwidth, and requests for the multipart upload requests and the associated parts of an object after the operation is completed. The point is you are charged when a multipart upload is completed (not aborted).

See also

▶ *Multipart Upload Overview* `https://docs.aws.amazon.com/AmazonS3/latest/dev/mpuoverview.html`

▶ *AWS SDK for Node.js* `http://docs.aws.amazon.com/AWSJavaScriptSDK/guide/node-intro.htm`

▶ Node.js S3 package npm `https://www.npmjs.com/package/s3`

▶ *Amazon Simple Storage Service: Introduction to Amazon S3* `http://docs.aws.amazon.com/AmazonS3/latest/dev/Introduction.html`

> ▸ *(PFC403) Maximizing Amazon S3 Performance | AWS re:Invent 2014* `http://www.slideshare.net/AmazonWebServices/pfc403-maximizing-amazon-s3-performance-aws-reinvent-2014`
>
> ▸ *AWS re:Invent 2014 | (PFC403) Maximizing Amazon S3 Performance* `https://www.youtube.com/watch?v=_FHRzq7eHQc`

How to optimize GET requests

To optimize GET requests, we can apply the same technique as with PUT requests. One is to parallelize GET requests, and the other is to use CloudFront to cache objects and reduce the number of GETs. This is because, as you already learned how the performance between S3 and CloudFront differs in *How to measure throughput between S3 and CloudFront* in the *Chapter 5, Distributing Your Contents via CloudFront*, CloudFront provides content with low-latency distributing for your content stored in your S3 bucket through a global network of edge locations.

We will see the difference of the performance using a simple `curl` command.

Getting ready

You need to complete the following set up in advance:

- ▸ Sign up on AWS and be able to access S3 with your IAM credentials
- ▸ Install and set up AWS CLI in your PC or use Amazon Linux AMI
- ▸ Create and enable a CloudFront distribution over your bucket following the instruction, *How to configure a CloudFront distribution on the Amazon S3 bucket* in *Chapter 5, Distributing Your Contents via CloudFront*

How to do it...

We download a 300 GB file through S3 bucket (S3 endpoint) and a CloudFront distribution (CloudFront domain) over HTTP using the curl command to compare the time.

The regions of EC2 instance and S3 bucket are the same as the previous section.

- ▸ **EC2 instance**: The Asia Pacific Tokyo region (ap-northeast-1)
- ▸ **S3 bucket**: The US Standard region (us-east-1)

First, we set up a sample shell script, and download the object through the S3 bucket and a CloudFront distribution using the script:

1. Put the following script and save the script as `s3_download.sh`:

```bash
#!/bin/bash

url=$1
thread=$2
part_name=$(basename ${url})
tmp_dir=/var/tmp
output_path=$PWD/${part_name}
content_length=$(curl -s -I ${url} | awk '/^Content-Length/
{print $2}' | strings)
range=$((${content_length} / ${thread}))
parts=
pids=

function show_log {
  echo "\$ $*"
  eval $*
}

echo "## Begin uploading."
num=0
while [ ${num} -lt ${thread} ]; do
  from=$((${range} * ${num}))
  if [ ${num} = $((${thread} -1 )) ]; then
    to=
  else
    to=$((${range} * $((${num} + 1)) - 1))
  fi
  part_path=${tmp_dir}/${part_name}.${num}

  show_log "curl -s -r ${from}-${to} -o ${part_path} ${url}
  &"
  pids="${pids} $!"
  parts="${parts} ${part_path}"
  num=$((${num} + 1))
done

echo "## Downloading objects in the background: ${pids}"
wait ${pids}
cat ${parts} > ${output_path}
echo "## Finished downloading."
```

```
        for part in ${parts}; do
          [ -f ${part} ] && rm -f ${part}
        done
```

How it works...

First of all, let's try downloading a 300 GB object through CloudFront with 10 threads. If it succeeds, we will download the same object changing the number of threads.

You can download an object and see how long it takes with the following command:

```
$ url=your-object-url
$ thread=number
$ time ./s3_download.sh ${url} ${thread}
```

The following example is to download an object from CloudFront with 10 threads, and it shows the following output:

```
$ url=http://djq4k263hnxvw.cloudfront.net/300mb.dmp
$ thread=10
$ time ./s3_download.sh ${url} ${thread}
## Begin uploading.
$ curl -s -r 0-78643199 -o /var/tmp/300mb.dmp.0
http://djq4k263hnxvw.cloudfront.net/300mb.dmp &
$ curl -s -r 78643200-157286399 -o /var/tmp/300mb.dmp.1
http://djq4k263hnxvw.cloudfront.net/300mb.dmp &
$ curl -s -r 157286400-235929599 -o /var/tmp/300mb.dmp.2
http://djq4k263hnxvw.cloudfront.net/300mb.dmp &
$ curl -s -r 235929600- -o /var/tmp/300mb.dmp.3
http://djq4k263hnxvw.cloudfront.net/300mb.dmp &
## Downloading objects in the background:  6026 6027 6028 6029
## Finished downloading.

real    0m11.086s
user    0m0.136s
sys     0m0.948s
```

As it took about 11 seconds to download the object, the transfer rate was 27.27 MB/sec.

Now, let's see the output when an object is downloaded directly from the S3 bucket:

```
$ url=http://s3.amazonaws.com/bucket-sample-us-east-1/300mb.dmp
$ thread=10
$ time ./s3_download.sh ${url} ${thread}
...
real    1m14.762s
user    0m0.372s
sys     0m1.428s
```

Now, let's see the summarization of each score. The following table shows the speed of CloudFront in different tests:

Thread	1	10	20	40	80
Range (Bytes)	314572800	31457280	15728640	7864320	3932160
Time (seconds)	13.40	11.08	12.26	14.91	17.57
Transfer Rate (MB)	23.48	28.39	25.66	21.10	17.90

The following table shows the speed test score of S3:

Thread	1	10	20	40	80
Range (Bytes)	314572800	31457280	15728640	7864320	3932160
Time (seconds)	139.88	74.76	21.37	18.84	18.00
Transfer Rate (MB)	2.25	4.21	14.72	16.70	17.48

To summarize, it is able to reduce the latency both by delivering your content via a CloudFront distribution and parallelizing GET requests. In detail, the score shows that CloudFront is much greater than S3 in the transfer rate and as the number of threads increases, the time grows. The S3 performance shows that the difference of the transfer rate between 40 and 80 threads is small, so CloudFront will be more effective for a single large object. Let's get to the conclusion:

- Parallelizing GET requests and multithread requests performs better when downloading objects
- Your application needs to be built with aligning parts of objects for parallelizing GET requests
- Parallelizing GET requests is effective for unreliable networks and for a large object

There's more...

There is another option to improve GET requests performance. Parallelizing GET requests improves GET request performance sending multiple requests. On the other hand, Range GET request is to specify ranges of bytes for a large object to download in smaller units.

Range GET request support

You learned that making multiple requests and using the `Range` request header improved the efficiency of downloading objects in smaller units. For example, if a CloudFront gets a `Range` GET request, it checks whether the cache stored in the edge location received the request. If the cache contains the whole object or the requested part of the object, the edge location immediately delivers the requested range from the cache.

On the other hand, if the cache does not contain the requested range, CloudFront forwards the request to your origin. In addition, CloudFront can request a larger range than the requested range in the `Range` GET to optimize performance. In short, the cache behavior of CloudFront differs as follows:

▶ If the origin supports the Range GET requests, it returns the requested range and CloudFront delivers the requested range. Also, CloudFront will have cached the requested range for the future in the edge location.

▶ If the origin does not support the Range GET requests, it returns the whole object and CloudFront delivers the whole object. Also, CloudFront will have cached the whole object for the future in the edge locations.

CloudFront follows the RFC specification for the Range header in general. However, if a range header request does not meet the following requirements, CloudFront will return an HTTP status code 200 with the full object instead of returning status code 206 with the specified range:

▶ The range must be listed in an ascending order, for example, 0-100, 200-300 is valid, but 200-300, 0-100 is invalid

▶ The ranges must not overlap, for example, 0-100, 50-150 is invalid

▶ All the ranges specifications must be valid

Finally, let's see the following example:

▶ The first example shows that the requested range is NOT listed in ascending order (200-300, 0-100) and returns a status code of 200:

```
$ curl -I -r 200-300, 0-100 http://djq4k263hnxvw.cloudfront.
net/300mb.dmp \
| egrep '^(HTTP/1.1|Content-Length|Accept-Ranges|Server|X-
Cache)'
HTTP/1.1 200 OK
Content-Length: 314572800
Accept-Ranges: bytes
Server: AmazonS3
X-Cache: Hit from cloudfront
```

▶ The second example shows that the other is listed in ascending order (0-100, 200-300) and returns a status code of 206:

```
$ curl -I -r 0-100,200-300 http://djq4k263hnxvw.cloudfront.
net/300mb.dmp \
| egrep '^(HTTP/1.1|Content-Length|Accept-Ranges|Server|X-Cache)'
HTTP/1.1 206 Partial Content
Content-Length: 521
Accept-Ranges: bytes
Server: AmazonS3
X-Cache: Hit from cloudfront
```

See also

- *Performance Optimization* `http://docs.aws.amazon.com/AmazonS3/latest/dev/PerformanceOptimization.html`

- *How CloudFront Processes Partial Requests for an Object (Range GETs)* `http://docs.aws.amazon.com/AmazonCloudFront/latest/DeveloperGuide/RangeGETs.html`

- *RF2616 Range Header* `http://www.w3.org/Protocols/rfc2616/rfc2616-sec14.html#sec14.35`

12
Creating Triggers and Notifying S3 Events to Lambda

In this chapter, you will take a look at the following recipes:

- ▶ How to create a sample policy to notify S3 events
- ▶ How to enable S3 event notification with Lambda

Introduction

Amazon S3 event notifications can publish event notifications when certain events occur in your bucket creating a notification configuration, for example, via Amazon SNS, Amazon SQS, or AWS Lambda. For instance, when a new object is uploaded in your bucket, Amazon S3 will send notifications to AWS Lambda and the event starts Lambda to process code as a Lambda function so that you can invoke a notification to your e-mail address or your mobile devices using an SNS topic. The point is, you do not need to implement your own system to monitor and notify events in order to detect changes of events because AWS Lambda automatically scales according to the rate of events. AWS Lambda also supports the use of its own custom code referred to as the Lambda function (λ) zipping and uploading your code to AWS Lambda.

The following screenshot shows a common application process of S3 event notifications with SNS topics, SQS queues, and Lambda functions:

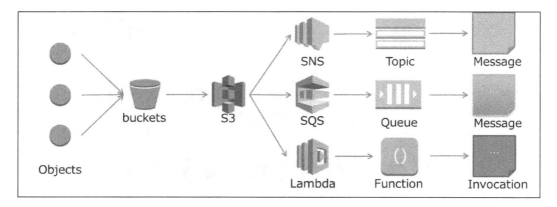

First, we will be creating an SNS topic and configure S3 event notification in a bucket in order to understand the S3 event notifications. After that, we will be learning a more practical example of executing a Lambda function triggered by S3 event notifications.

How to create a sample policy to notify S3 events

First, we will be creating an SNS through the management console to send an e-mail to your address and S3 event notifications to receive notifications when objects have been uploaded to your S3 bucket. Before moving to the *How to do it...* section, let's quickly see what Amazon **Simple Notification Service (SNS)** is.

Amazon SNS is a web service used to send messages to subscribing endpoints or clients, and consists of two clients, publishers, and subscribers as shown in the following diagram:

- ▶ Publishers asynchronously correspond with subscribers by sending messages to SNS topics
- ▶ Subscribers (for example, web servers, e-mail addresses, Amazon SQS queues, and AWS Lambda functions) receive the message or notification over one of the supported protocols (for example, Amazon SQS, HTTP/S, SMS, and Lambda)

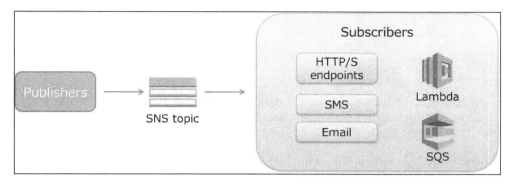

Amazon SNS pricing is based on the number of notifications you publish, the number of notifications you deliver, and additional API calls for requests. The notification pricing varies by endpoint type.

The pricing of publishing is summarized as follows:

▶ The first 1 million Amazon SNS requests per month are free.

▶ $0.50 per 1 million Amazon SNS requests thereafter.

▶ Amazon SNS allows a maximum limit of 256 KB for published messages. Each 64 KB chunk of published data is calculated as 1 request and a single API call with a 256 KB payload will be calculated as four requests.

The pricing of notification summarizes as follows:

▶ Mobile push notification costs $0.50 per million requests and 1 million requests per month are free

▶ E-mail/E-mail-JSON costs $2.00 per 100,000 requests and 1,000 requests per month are free

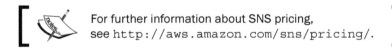

For further information about SNS pricing, see http://aws.amazon.com/sns/pricing/.

Getting ready

You do not have to request permissions to use S3 event notifications. All you need to do is:

▶ Prepare an e-mail address to send notifications

▶ Sign up on AWS and access S3 and SNS with your IAM credentials

▶ Create a bucket following the instruction from *Chapter 1, Managing Common Operations with AWS SDKs*

As your S3 bucket and your SNS topic must belong to the same region, make sure that you choose the same region when you create the resources.

How to do it...

Now, let's create an SNS topic and a subscription, and confirm the subscription with your e-mail address. After finishing configuring SNS topics, we enable S3 event notifications and confirm that an event has been notified by uploading an object in your bucket.

The following instruction uses the US standard region:

1. Sign in to the AWS management console and move to the SNS console at `https://console.aws.amazon.com/sns/`.

2. Click on **Get Started**:

3. In the **SNS Home** panel on the right, click on **Create topic**:

4. Enter the topic name in the **Topic name** box and then click on **Create topic**:

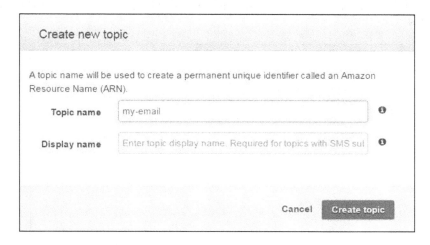

- ❑ The topic name must be up to 256 alphanumeric characters and hyphens (-) and underscores (_) are allowed
- ❑ The display name is required for SMS subscriptions and can be up to 10 characters

5. Select the topic you created, and choose **Subscribe to topic** from the **Actions** button:

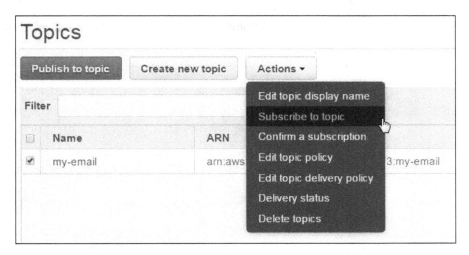

6. Choose **Email** in the **Protocol** box, and enter your e-mail address in the **Endpoint** box, and then click on **Create subscription**. Copy or write down the topic ARN in the **Topic ARN** box:

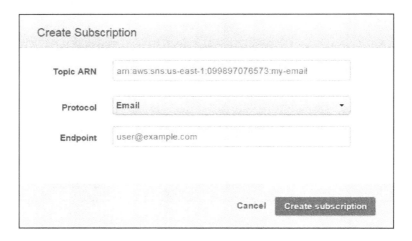

 Amazon Resource Names (**ARNs**) is a unique identification to specify a resource across all AWS resources. For more information, see `http://docs.aws.amazon.com/general/latest/gr/aws-arns-and-namespaces.html/`.

7. You can see the **Subscription ID** column, which becomes **PendingConfirmation** as shown in the following screenshot:

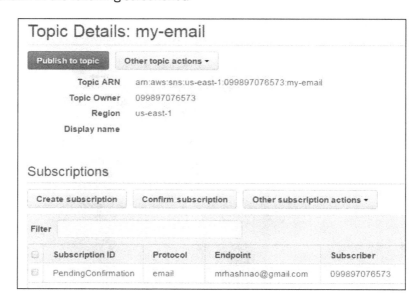

8. Check your e-mail box, and you will be receiving an e-mail immediately as shown in the following screenshot. Click on **Confirm subscription**:

9. After clicking on **Confirm subscription**, the following pop-up appears and the subscription confirmed, as shown in the following screenshot:

10. You can see the **Subscription ID** column confirmed in the SNS console, as shown in the following screenshot:

11. Select the topic you created and choose **Edit topic policy** from the **Actions** button:

12. Click on **Advanced View**, add the following topic policy statement in the original policy, and click on **Update policy**:

  ❏ The `Sid` policy statement to add is written in red

  ❏ Replace `topic-arn` with the topic ARN you created

  ❏ Replace `your-bucket` with the bucket name you created

"Resource": "topic-arn" and "AWS:SourceOwner": "aws-account-id" in the "__default_statement_ID" Sid, are supposed to be defined with the default value:

```
{
  "Version": "2008-10-17",
  "Id": "__default_policy_ID",
  "Statement": [
    {
      "Sid": "__default_statement_ID",
      "Effect": "Allow",
      "Principal": {
        "AWS": "*"
      },
      "Action": [
        "SNS:Publish",
        "SNS:RemovePermission",
        "SNS:SetTopicAttributes",
        "SNS:DeleteTopic",
        "SNS:ListSubscriptionsByTopic",
        "SNS:GetTopicAttributes",
        "SNS:Receive",
```

```
          "SNS:AddPermission",
          "SNS:Subscribe"
        ],
        "Resource": "topic-arn",
        "Condition": {
          "StringEquals": {
            "AWS:SourceOwner": "aws-account-id"
          }
        }
      },
      {
        "Sid": "s3-event-notification",
        "Effect": "Allow",
        "Principal": {
          "AWS": "*"
        },
        "Action": "SNS:Publish",
        "Resource": "topic-arn",
        "Condition": {
          "ArnLike": {
            "aws:SourceArn": "arn:aws:s3:*:*:your-bucket"
          }
        }
      }
    ]
  }
```

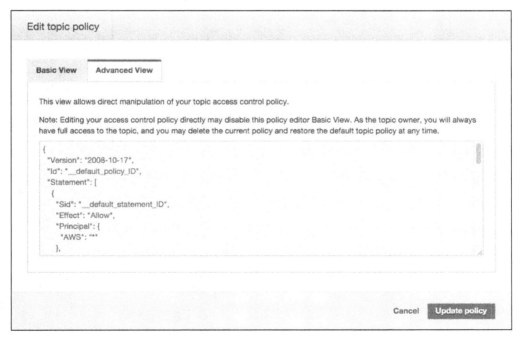

13. Select the topic you created, and then click on **Publish to topic**:

14. Fill in the following box, and then click on **Publish message**:

❑ Enter the subject name in the **Subject** box

❑ Choose **Raw** in the **Message** format

❑ Enter the message in the **Message** box

❑ Input the TTL value in seconds in the **Time to live (TTL)** box

15. Check your e-mail box, and you will be receiving an e-mail immediately as shown in the following screenshot:

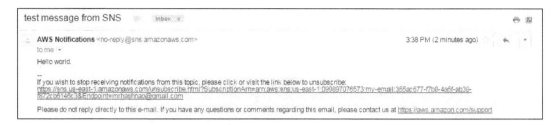

16. Next, move to the S3 console at `https://console.aws.amazon.com/sns/`.

17. In the S3 console, click on the bucket name and then on **Events** from the **Properties** tab:

18. Enter and choose the following, and then click on **Save**:

   ❑ Enter a descriptive name in the **Name** box. If left as blank, a GUID will be generated for the name.

❑ Select a value in the **Events** box, as shown in the following screenshot—you can create only one notification per event type per bucket:

❑ Choose **SNS topic** in the **Send To** section

❑ Choose `Add SNS topic ARN` in the **SNS topic** box

❑ Enter the topic ARN in the **SNS topic ARN** box

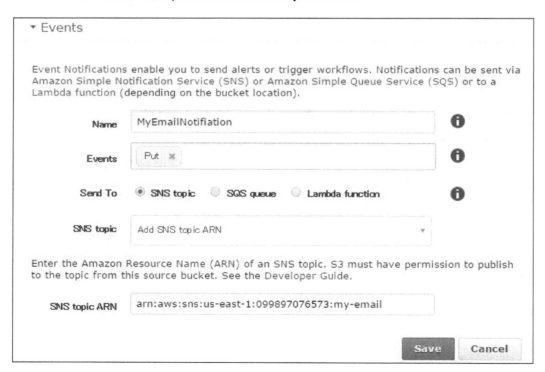

19. You can see the notification as shown in the following screenshot:

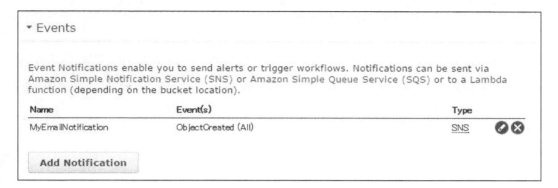

How it works...

As we have finished setting up an SNS topic and S3 event notification, let's try to upload an object in your bucket and see the notification sent to your address. Here, we will be using AWS CLI S3 subcommand to upload an object and confirm whether the object is uploaded:

```
$ bucket=your-bucket
$ key=sns_test.txt
$ echo "hello world." > ${key}
$ aws s3 cp ${key} s3://${bucket}/
$ aws s3 ls s3://${bucket}/${key}
```

Check your e-mail address and you will be receiving an e-mail immediately, as shown in the following screenshot:

When you receive the message, you will feel it hard to read and understand the text at a glance because the message is shown in one-liner in the JSON format as shown earlier. I put the message formatted in JSON format as follows:

```json
{
  "Records": [
    {
      "eventVersion": "2.0",
      "eventSource": "aws:s3",
      "awsRegion": "us-east-1",
      "eventTime": "2015-04-13T07:06:33.244Z",
      "eventName": "ObjectCreated:Put",
      "userIdentity": {
        "principalId": "AWS:AIDAIR5WEOKJZ7LIIWV3E"
      },
      "requestParameters": {
        "sourceIPAddress": "xxx.xxx.xxx.xxx"
      },
      "responseElements": {
        "x-amz-request-id": "D94624D5EEF4DDCC",
        "x-amz-id-2":
        "OT657fuyFtSRSap2GBKcOyrfSGnXdmV5/
        p4oe1WmqjoeE0w8bX8BZdxCjLV6YHtuz26uxcikjXg="
      },
      "s3": {
        "s3SchemaVersion": "1.0",
        "configurationId": "MyEmailNotification",
        "bucket": {
          "name": "your-bucket",
          "ownerIdentity": {
            "principalId": "A20MZKPR0T2FD6"
          },
          "arn": "arn:aws:s3:::your-bucket"
        },
        "object": {
          "key": "sns_test.txt",
          "size": 13,
          "eTag": "fa093de5fc603823f08524f9801f0546"
        }
      }
    }
  ]
}
```

See also

▶ *Configuring Amazon S3 Event Notifications* is available at `https://docs.aws.amazon.com/AmazonS3/latest/dev/NotificationHowTo.html`

▶ *Event Message Structure* is available at `https://docs.aws.amazon.com/AmazonS3/latest/dev/notification-content-structure.html`

How to enable S3 event notification with Lambda

Amazon Lambda also supports to run custom code referred as Lambda function by directly inputting your code or uploading a compressed ZIP file of the code in order to run your application code. Amazon Lambda processes your Lambda functions in response to events, for example, the object-created events in S3 bucket, the DynamoDB table updates, or JSON inputs or HTTP commands from your application.

> AWS Lambda supports Java and Node.js. For more information, see `http://aws.amazon.com/lambda/details/`.

We will be creating a sample Node.js. S3 notifies an event to AWS Lambda and AWS Lambda invokes a Lambda function, which then creates a thumbnail and saves it to a target bucket when the objects (image files) are uploaded into a source bucket. The following screenshot shows the sample application architecture composed of a Lambda function, IAM role, and S3 bucket.

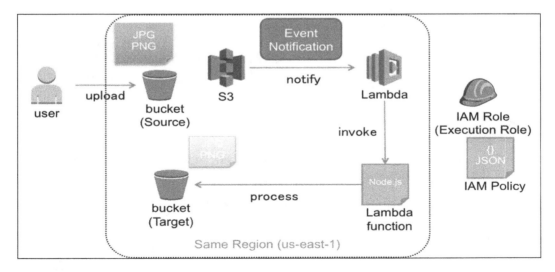

Getting ready

Lambda currently supports the following regions on its preview on April 14, 2015. Since your S3 bucket and Lambda must belong to the same region, make sure that you choose the same region when you create the resources:

- US Standard (N. Virginia)
- US West (Oregon)
- EU (Ireland)

The other factors you need to prepare in advance are as follows:

- Sign up to AWS and access all the AWS resources (administrative privileges) with your IAM credentials and write down the IAM user's credentials. These IAM credentials are necessary to create the Lambda function with AWS CLI.

> For further information about how to create the administrative group, create an IAM user, and add the user to the group. Refer to the *Walkthrough 4: Bucket and user policy examples* recipe from *Chapter 6, Securing Resources with Bucket Policies and IAM*.

- Install and set up AWS CLI on your PC or use Amazon Linux AMI. AWS CLI 1.7.22 or later is required because the AWS Lambda create function option is implemented with the latest version.

> For further information about how to set up AWS CLI, see
> `http://docs.aws.amazon.com/cli/latest/userguide/installing.html`.

- Install Node.js, following the instructions given in the *Learning AWS SDK for Node.js and basic S3 operations with sample code* recipe from *Chapter 1, Managing Common Operations with AWS SDKs*.

How to do it...

We will be creating a sample Lambda function and verifying the sample Lambda function, following the process as follows:

- Create two S3 buckets (source and target) and upload a sample object
- Create a Lambda function deployment package
- Create an IAM role (execution role)

▶ Upload the deployment package and test it

▶ Configure Amazon S3 to publish events

▶ Upload an object and verify whether a thumbnail of the object is created

To create an S3 bucket, perform the following steps:

1. Add a named profile for the administrator user in the CLI config:

```
$ cat >> ~/.aws/config <<EOF
[profile admin]
aws_access_key_id = administrator user access key ID
aws_access_key_id = administrator user secret access key
region = your-region
EOF
```

2. Create two S3 buckets:

```
$ source=your-source-bucket
$ target=your-target-bucket
$ aws s3api create-bucket --bucket ${source} --profile admin
$ aws s3api create-bucket --bucket ${target} --profile admin
```

3. Upload a sample object to the source bucket:

```
$ key=sample.jpg
$ aws s3 cp ${key} s3://${source} --profile admin
$ aws s3 ls s3://${bucket}/${key} --profile admin
```

4. Delete the sample object:

```
$ aws s3 rm s3://${source}/${key} --profile admin
```

To configure the Lambda function and test the function, perform the following steps:

1. Create a directory and a subdirectory:

```
$ mkdir -p uploader/node_modules
$ cd uploader/
```

2. Install the libraries:

```
$ npm install async gm
```

3. Copy the following example code and save it as CreateThumbnail.js in the uploader directory and replace dstBucket = "your-target-bucket" with the target bucket name:

```
// dependencies
var async = require('async');
var AWS = require('aws-sdk');
var gm = require('gm')
```

```
                .subClass({ imageMagick: true }); // Enable
                ImageMagick integration.
    var util = require('util');
    // constants
    var MAX_WIDTH  = 100;
    var MAX_HEIGHT = 100;
    // get reference to S3 client
    var s3 = new AWS.S3();
    exports.handler = function(event, context) {
            // Read options from the event.
            console.log("Reading options from event:\n",
            util.inspect(event, {depth:5}));
            var srcBucket = event.Records[0].s3.bucket.name;
            // Object key may have spaces or unicode non-ASCII
            characters.
        var srcKey =
        decodeURIComponent(event.Records[0].s3.object.key
        .replace(/\+/g, " "));
            var dstBucket = "your-target-bucket";
            var dstKey    = "thumbnail-" + srcKey;
            // Sanity check: validate that source and
            destination are different buckets.
            if (srcBucket == dstBucket) {
              console.error("Destination bucket must not match
              source bucket.");
            return;
            }
            // Infer the image type.
            var typeMatch = srcKey.match(/\.([^.]*)$/);
            if (!typeMatch) {
              console.error('unable to infer image type for key
              ' + srcKey);
            return;
            }
            var imageType = typeMatch[1];
            if (imageType != "jpg" && imageType != "png") {
              console.log('skipping non-image ' + srcKey);
            return;
            }
            // Download the image from S3, transform, and
            upload to a different S3bucket.
            async.waterfall([
              function download(next) {
                // Download the image from S3 into a buffer.
                  s3.getObject({
```

```
          Bucket: srcBucket,
          Key: srcKey
        },
      next);
    },
    function tranform(response, next) {
      gm(response.Body).size(function(err, size) {
        // Infer the scaling factor to avoid
        stretching the imageunnaturally.
        var scalingFactor = Math.min(
        MAX_WIDTH / size.width,
        MAX_HEIGHT / size.height
        );
        var width  = scalingFactor * size.width;
        var height = scalingFactor * size.height;
        // Transform the image buffer in memory.
        this.resize(width, height)
        .toBuffer(imageType, function(err, buffer) {
          if (err) {
            next(err);
          } else {
            next(null, response.ContentType,
            buffer);
          }
        });
      });
    },
    function upload(contentType, data, next) {
      // Stream the transformed image to a different
      S3 bucket.
      s3.putObject({
        Bucket: dstBucket,
        Key: dstKey,
        Body: data,
        ContentType: contentType
      },
    next);
  }
], function (err) {
    if (err) {
        console.error('Unable to resize ' + srcBucket
        + '/' + srcKey + ' and upload to ' + dstBucket
        + '/' + dstKey + ' due to an error: ' + err);
    } else {
```

```
                        console.log('Successfully resized ' + srcBucket
                        + '/' + srcKey + ' and uploaded to ' +
                        dstBucket + '/' + dstKey);
                }
            context.done();
        }
    );
};
```

4. Zip the Lambda script and the modules as `CreateThumbnail.zip`:

    ```
    $ function_name=CreateThumbnail
    $ zip -r ${function_name}.zip ${function_name}.js node_modules
    ```

    Make sure that you specify the Lambda script and the module directory. If you archive the directory itself (for example, `zip -r uploader/`), Lambda will not be able to find the module.

5. Create the following IAM policy file in JSON format and save it as `${role_name}.json`:

    ```
    {
        "Version": "2012-10-17",
        "Statement": [
            {
                "Effect": "Allow",
                "Action": "sts:AssumeRole",
                "Principal": {
                    "Service": "lambda.amazonaws.com"
                }
            }
        ]
    }
    ```

6. Create an IAM role to grant AWS Lambda permissions to assume the role.

    ```
    $ role_name=lambda_execution
    $ aws iam create-role --profile admin \
    --role-name ${role_name} \
    --assume-role-policy-document file://${role_name}.json
    ```

7. Write down the IAM role ARN that the preceding command outputs. If the command succeeds, it outputs as in the following message in the JSON format:

    ```
    {
        "Role": {
            "AssumeRolePolicyDocument": {
                "Version": "2012-10-17",
    ```

```
            "Statement": [
                {
                    "Action": "sts:AssumeRole",
                    "Effect": "Allow",
                    "Principal": {
                        "Service": "lambda.amazonaws.com"
                    }
                }
            ]
        },
        "RoleId": "AROAIMBYYBY5ZWH3BSOVM",
        "CreateDate": "2015-04-14T01:11:54.798Z",
        "RoleName": "lambda_execution",
        "Path": "/",
        "Arn": "arn:aws:iam::__AccountID__:role/lambda_execution"
    }
}
```

The IAM role ARN is needed when creating a Lambda function.

8. Attach an IAM policy `AWSLambdaExecute` to the role:

```
$ policy_arn=arn:aws:iam::aws:policy/AWSLambdaExecute
$ aws iam attach-role-policy --profile admin \
--role-name ${role_name} \
--policy-arn ${policy_arn}
```

9. You can also check the policy ARN of `AWSLambdaExecute` using the following command:

```
$ aws iam list-policies | \
jq '.Policies[] | select(.PolicyName == "AWSLambdaExecute")'
{
  "PolicyName": "AWSLambdaExecute",
  "CreateDate": "2015-02-06T18:40:46Z",
  "AttachmentCount": 0,
  "IsAttachable": true,
  "PolicyId": "ANPAJE5FX7FQZSU5XAKGO",
  "DefaultVersionId": "v1",
  "Path": "/",
  "Arn": "arn:aws:iam::aws:policy/AWSLambdaExecute",
  "UpdateDate": "2015-02-06T18:40:46Z"
}
```

10. Verify whether the user can reach AWS Lambda:

```
$ aws lambda list-functions --profile admin
```

If the command succeeds, it outputs as shown in the following message in the JSON format:

```json
{
    "Functions": [
        {
            "FunctionName": "CreateThumbnail",
            "MemorySize": 1024,
            "CodeSize": 87725,
            "FunctionArn": "arn:aws:lambda:us-east-1:__AccountID__
:function:CreateThumbnail",
            "Handler": "CreateThumbnail.handler",
            "Role": "arn:aws:iam::__AccountID__:role/lambda_
execution",
            "Timeout": 10,
            "LastModified": "2015-04-14T03:02:17.889+0000",
            "Runtime": "nodejs",
            "Description": ""
        }
    ]
}
```

11. Create a Lambda function. Make sure that you set the role_arn variable as IAM role ARN:

```
$ region=your-region
$ role_arn=IAM role ARN
$ function_name=CreateThumbnail
$ aws lambda create-function --profile admin \
--region ${region} \
--function-name ${function_name} \
--zip-file fileb://${function_name}.zip \
--role ${role_arn} \
--handler ${function_name}.handler \
--runtime nodejs \
--timeout 10 \
--memory-size 1024
```

12. Write down the function ARN that the preceding command outputs. If the command succeeds, it outputs as shown in the following message in JSON format:

```json
{
    "FunctionName": "CreateThumbnail",
    "CodeSize": 84233,
    "MemorySize": 1024,
    "FunctionArn": "arn:aws:lambda:us-east-1:__AccountID__:functio
n:CreateThumbnail",
    "Handler": "CreateThumbnail.handler",
    "Role": "arn:aws:iam::099897076573:role/lambda_execution",
    "Timeout": 10,
```

```
        "LastModified": "2015-04-15T01:57:08.256+0000",
        "Runtime": "nodejs",
        "Description": ""
}
```

The function ARN is needed when adding notification configuration to your Amazon S3 bucket later.

If you need to update your code, you can update the function code with the following command:

```
$ aws lambda update-function-code --profile admin \
--function-name ${function_name} \
--zip-file fileb://${function_name}.zip
```

To configure a notification on the bucket, perform the following steps:

1. Add permission to the Lambda function access policy. Make sure that you set the `bucket_owner_account_id` variable as your AWS account ID.

```
$ bucket_owner_account_id=bucket owner AWS account ID
$ aws lambda add-permission --profile admin \
--function-name ${function_name} \
--region ${region} \
--statement-id Id-x \
--action "lambda:InvokeFunction" \
--principal s3.amazonaws.com \
--source-arn arn:aws:s3:::${source} \
--source-account ${bucket_owner_account_id}
```

2. Verify whether the access policy is configured:

```
$ aws lambda get-policy --profile admin \
--function-name ${function_name}
```

If the command succeeds, it outputs as shown in the following message in JSON format:

```
{
    "Policy": "{\"Statement\":[{\"Condition\":{\"StringEquals\":{\
"AWS:Sourc
eAccount\":\"099897076573\"},\"ArnLike\":{\"AWS:SourceArn\":\"
arn:aws:s3:::your-source-
bucket\"}},\"Resource\":\"arn:aws:lambda:us-east-
1:__AccountID__:function:CreateThumbnail\",\"Action\":\"lambda
:InvokeFunction\",\"Principal\":{\"Service\":\"s3.amazonaws.co
m\"},\"Sid\":\"Id-
x\",\"Effect\":\"Allow\"}],\"Id\":\"default\",\"Version\":\"20
12-10-17\"}"
}
```

3. Create the following notification in JSON format and save it as ${notification_ configuration}.json. Make sure to replace Function ARN with the Lambda function ARN:

```
{
   "LambdaFunctionConfigurations": [{
      "Id": "CreateThumbnail",
      "LambdaFunctionArn": "Function ARN",
      "Events": [
         "s3:ObjectCreated:Put"
      ]
   }]
}
```

4. Configure the notification on the bucket:

```
$ aws s3api put-bucket-notification-configuration --profile admin \
--bucket ${source} \
--notification-configuration
file://${notification_configuration}.json
```

5. Verify whether the notification is applied on the bucket:

```
$ aws s3api get-bucket-notification-configuration --profile admin \
--bucket ${source} \
```

If the command succeeds, it outputs as shown in the following message in JSON format:

```
{
    "LambdaFunctionConfigurations": [
        {
            "LambdaFunctionArn": "arn:aws:lambda:us-east-1:__Accou
ntID__:function:CreateThumbnail",
            "Id": "CreateThumbnail",
            "Events": [
                "s3:ObjectCreated:Put"
            ]
        }
    ]
}
```

How it works...

Now that we have configured the S3 bucket, the Lambda function, the IAM role for Lambda function, and the S3 event notification, let's see how the Lambda function works by uploading a sample object into your bucket and describing the logging via CloudWatch.

 CloudWatch is a monitoring service that AWS provides in order to collect and monitor metrics of AWS resources. For more information, refer to `http://aws.amazon.com/cloudwatch/`.

First, put the object in your source bucket using the following command; the object file must be JPG or PNG:

```
$ key=sample.jpg
$ aws s3 cp ${key} s3://${source} --profile admin
```

Next, you can see that a thumbnail of the object is created in the target bucket immediately:

```
$ aws s3 ls s3://${target}
2015-04-15 03:25:01       4808 thumbnail-sample.jpg
```

There's more...

Lastly, we trace the event of the Lambda function by calling CloudWatch Logs API. We need to take a few steps to get to the event.

1. Describe the log groups and write down the `logGroupName` of the Lambda function:

    ```
    $ aws logs describe-log-groups
    {
        "logGroups": [
            {
                "arn": "arn:aws:logs:us-east-1:099897076573:log-
                group:/aws/lambda/CreateThumbnail:*",
                "creationTime": 1428981392334,
                "metricFilterCount": 0,
                "logGroupName": "/aws/lambda/CreateThumbnail",
                "storedBytes": 10042
            }
        ]
    }
    ```

2. Describe log streams and write down the `logStreamName`:

    ```
    $ logGroupName=Log Group Name
    $ aws logs describe-log-streams \
    ```

```
--log-group-name ${logGroupName} \
--order-by LastEventTime --descending --limit 1 |\
jq -r '.logStreams[].logStreamName'
```

If the command succeeds, it outputs as shown in the following message:

```
2015/04/15/9805c070b09a4e4dab947ccdc039fdc6
```

3. Get the log event specifying the LogStreamName:

```
$ logStreamName=Log Stream Name
$ aws logs get-log-events \
--log-group-name ${logGroupName} \
--log-stream-name ${logStreamName}
```

If the command succeeds, it outputs as shown in the following message in JSON format:

```
{
    "nextForwardToken": "f/3186928803066775588207221579450786249870
0093980120239093",
    "events": [
        {
            "ingestionTime": 1429068313796,
            "timestamp": 1429068298753,
            "message": "START RequestId: fdc15f3d-e31e-11e4-
            94fd-bff938049177\n"
        },
    ...
    "nextBackwardToken": "b/3186928800178829084997505882621910733
5621311650957754368"
}
```

See also

► *Example Walkthrough 2: Configure a Bucket for Notifications (Message Destination: AWS Lambda)* is available at https://docs.aws.amazon.com/AmazonS3/latest/dev/notification-walkthrough-2.html

► *What is AWS Lambda* is available at http://docs.aws.amazon.com/lambda/latest/dg/welcome.html

Index

Thank you for buying
Amazon S3 Cookbook

About Packt Publishing

Packt, pronounced 'packed', published its first book, *Mastering phpMyAdmin for Effective MySQL Management*, in April 2004, and subsequently continued to specialize in publishing highly focused books on specific technologies and solutions.

Our books and publications share the experiences of your fellow IT professionals in adapting and customizing today's systems, applications, and frameworks. Our solution-based books give you the knowledge and power to customize the software and technologies you're using to get the job done. Packt books are more specific and less general than the IT books you have seen in the past. Our unique business model allows us to bring you more focused information, giving you more of what you need to know, and less of what you don't.

Packt is a modern yet unique publishing company that focuses on producing quality, cutting-edge books for communities of developers, administrators, and newbies alike. For more information, please visit our website at www.PacktPub.com.

About Packt Enterprise

In 2010, Packt launched two new brands, Packt Enterprise and Packt Open Source, in order to continue its focus on specialization. This book is part of the Packt Enterprise brand, home to books published on enterprise software – software created by major vendors, including (but not limited to) IBM, Microsoft, and Oracle, often for use in other corporations. Its titles will offer information relevant to a range of users of this software, including administrators, developers, architects, and end users.

Writing for Packt

We welcome all inquiries from people who are interested in authoring. Book proposals should be sent to author@packtpub.com. If your book idea is still at an early stage and you would like to discuss it first before writing a formal book proposal, then please contact us; one of our commissioning editors will get in touch with you.

We're not just looking for published authors; if you have strong technical skills but no writing experience, our experienced editors can help you develop a writing career, or simply get some additional reward for your expertise.

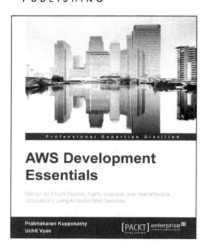

AWS Development Essentials

ISBN: 9978-1-78217-361-8   Paperback: 226 pages

Design and build flexible, highly scalable, and cost-effective applications using Amazon Web Services

1. Integrate and use AWS services in an application.

2. Reduce the development time and billing cost using the AWS billing and management console.

3. This is a fast-paced tutorial that will cover application deployment using various tools along with best practices for working with AWS services.

OpenStack Essentials

ISBN: 978-1-78398-708-5   Paperback: 182 pages

Demystify the cloud by building your own private OpenStack cloud

1. Set up a powerful cloud platform using OpenStack.

2. Learn about the components of OpenStack and how they interact with each other.

3. Follow a step-by-step process that exposes the inner details of an OpenStack cluster.

Please check **www.PacktPub.com** for information on our titles

Implementing Cloud Storage with OpenStack Swift

ISBN: 978-1-78216-805-8   Paperback: 140 pages

Design, implement, and successfully manage your own cloud storage cluster using the popular OpenStack Swift software

1. Learn about the fundamentals of cloud storage using OpenStack Swift.

2. Explore how to install and manage OpenStack Swift along with various hardware and tuning options.

3. Perform data transfer and management using REST APIs.

OpenStack Cloud Computing Cookbook
Second Edition

ISBN: 978-1-78216-758-7   Paperback: 396 pages

Over 100 recipes to successfully set up and manage your OpenStack cloud environments with complete coverage of Nova, Swift, Keystone, Glance, Horizon, Neutron, and Cinder

1. Updated for OpenStack Grizzly.

2. Learn how to install, configure, and manage all of the OpenStack core projects including new topics like block storage and software defined networking.

3. Learn how to build your Private Cloud utilizing DevOps and Continuous Integration tools and techniques.

Please check **www.PacktPub.com** for information on our titles